ISSUES IN MARXIST PHILOSOPHY

Volume I

DIALECTICS AND METHOD

ISSUES IN MARXIST PHILOSOPHY

Volume I
DIALECTICS AND METHOD

EDITED BY
JOHN MEPHAM
AND
DAVID-HILLEL RUBEN

HUMANITIES PRESS

First published in the United States in 1979 by
HUMANITIES PRESS INC.,
Atlantic Highlands, New Jersey 07716

© The Harvester Press Limited, 1979

Library of Congress Cataloging in Publication Data

Main entry under title:
Issues in Marxist philosophy.
   (Marxist theory and contemporary capitalism)
   CONTENTS: v. 1. Dialectics and method. – v.
   2. Materialism. – v.   3. Epistemology, science, ideology.
   1. Dialectical materialism – Addresses, essays,
   lectures.   2. Marx, Karl, 1818–1883 – Addresses, essays,
   lectures.   3. Historical materialism – Addresses, essays,
   lectures.   I. Mepham, John, 1938–   II. Ruben,
   David-Hillel.   III. Series.
   B809.8.I774   1979   146′.3   79–12173

   ISBN 0-391-00934-6 (v. 1)
   ISBN 0-391-01017-4 pbk.

Photosetting by Thomson Press (India) Ltd., New Delhi
and printed in Great Britain by
Redwood Burn Limited, Trowbridge and Esher

Contents

Notes on Authors: Volume I

SCOTT MEIKLE studied philosophy at Bristol University from 1960 to 1963, and at Balliol College, Oxford from 1963–1965. Since then he has lectured in philosophy at Glasgow University..He is an editor of, and contributor to, the journal *Critique*: he has written on 'Reasons for Action', *Philosophical Quaterly*, 1973, and on 'Aristotle's Political Economy of the Polis', *Journal of Hellenic Studies*, forthcoming.

DAVID-HILLEL RUBEN is Lecturer in Philosophy at the University of Essex, and has previously held appointments at the Universities of Glasgow and Edinburgh. He was born in Chicago, and took his B.A. from Darmouth College and his Ph.D. from Harvard. His articles have appeared in *The Philosophical Quarterly*, *Analysis*, *Critique*, *Philosophy and Phenomenological Research*, *The Monist*, *Ethics* and other journals. He is author of *Marxism and Materialism: A Study in Marxist Theory of Knowledge*.

CHRIS ARTHUR is a lecturer in Philosophy at the University of Sussex. He studied at Nottingham and Oxford. He brought out an edition of Marx and Engels' *German Ideology*, and edited a translation of E. B. Pashukanis' *General Theory of Law and Marxism*. He has participated in the radical philosophy movement, and in the editing of its journal *Radical Philosophy*, from its foundation.

MILTON FISK was born in Kentucky. He took a B.S. at the University of Notre Dame in 1953 and a Ph.D. at Yale in 1958. He has taught at Notre Dame and Yale, and is now Professor of Philosophy at Indiana University. His interests are in the metaphysics of nature and in social and political philosophy. He has published articles in numerous journals and is the author of *A Modern Formal Logic* (1964), *Nature and Necessity: An Essay in Physical Ontology* (1973) and *Socialism from Below in the United States* (1977).

JOHN MEPHAM studied biochemistry at Oxford and the history and philosophy of science at Princeton. He has taught philosophy at the University of Sussex and at Reed College in Oregon. He has published articles on Aristotle, Van Helmont, Lévi-Strauss, Althusser and Marx. Since resigning from university teaching in 1976 he has worked as a translator (of Koyré, Gorz, Jakobson and Foucault) and as an editor. He was a member of the Brighton Labour Process Group of the Conference of Socialist Economists. His main intellectual interest is now in the poetics of the novel and he wrote 'Figures of Desire: Narration and Fiction in *To the Lighthouse*' for *The Modern English Novel* (ed.) G. D. Josipovici (1976). He is at present writing about poetics and the modern French novel with a grant from the South East Arts Association.

General Introduction

THE essays in these Volumes on issues in Marxist philosophy are all by authors from English-speaking countries. With only three exceptions, they are printed here for the first time. In these countries, we have had to struggle over the years with the task of reading and evaluating the works of important continental European philosophers, both Marxists and non-Marxists, and of questioning our own distance from them. We have had to ask what specific contributions our relations to various English-speaking philosophical traditions can make to the advancement of Marxist philosophy, philosophical traditions to which we are essentially related even when the character of that relation is in many fundamental ways a critical one. Much Marxist philosophical writing in the English-speaking world over the last decade has been more or less confined to exegesis and assimilation of continental philosophical systems; Sartre and the Frankfurt School, Lukacs and Korsch, Gramsci and della Volpe, more recently Althusser, Colletti, and Timpanaro. It will be clear to the reader of these present Volumes that these philosophers have exerted an important influence on their contents. These essays are not written in defiant ignorance or xenophobic dismissal of their work; on the contrary, we respect them by our attention to what they can teach us and by our attempt to make our own distinctive contribution to Marxist philosophy.

Thus, we think that the time is ripe for going beyond the rather passive assimilation of continental European philosophy that has hitherto dominated the Marxist intellectual landscape in the English-speaking world. Many English-speaking philosophers are ready to make their own contributions in areas of philosophical discussion in which, in spite of the volume of writing produced by French, German, and Italian Marxist philosophers, the state of the debate is still one of the utmost confusion. Many of us have the sense that the philosophical argument has not been nearly deep enough, has not made sufficiently deep contact with the really fundamental philosophical issues, and that Marxist positions on central philosophical issues are still quite crude and superficial. Very often, argument and discussion have not been pursued at an abstract enough level, or with sufficient persistence and tenacity. Sometimes Marxist philosophers write as if they must select one of a small number of possible answers to some central issue or difficulty, without exploring all the possible options or alternatives open. Marxist philosophy can only advance if it reaches down to the most general and abstract of philosophical categories, by the methods of sustained, persistent discussion and rational argument. English-speaking philosophers have a distinctive role to play here and we hope that these Volumes of essays will show that this is so.

These essays are not written by a group of philosophers who in any sense constitute a school setting up a new system of doctrine, a new catechism of truths, let alone reviving any old ones, although they are all written from within a classical Marxist orientation. Two of the essays in these Volumes were written more or less directly under the influence of Althusser, although they are very selective in what they take from his work and are not at all expositions of Althusserian positions. In many of the other essays, the figures of Althusser, Lukacs, Colletti, and Timpanaro appear as worthy opponents, and an attempt is made to open up discussion in a way that is distinctive and which draws more on the English-speaking philosophical virtues of disciplined argument and attention to detailed elaboration and defence of one's own positions.

Overall, a certain coherence of direction emerges from these essays. The reader will notice, first, the persistent appearance of realist categories (potentiality, natural or physical necessity, natural kinds, essence and appearance), some of which derive from the Aristotelian tradition, and all of which indicate, negatively, the deeply non-empiricist or non-positivist ontology and epistemology that dominates these volumes. Marxist philosophy, since its inception, has been driven between the Scylla of positivism and the Charybdis of idealism (usually of a 'humanist' variety). On the one side were figures such as Plekhanov, Engels, Dietzgen, Lenin, Bogdanov, and many writers of the period of the Second

International; on the other, stood Lukacs, Deborin, the Frankfurt School, Korsch, Sartre, and various 'humanist' Marxist tendencies. Some, from the Austro-Marxists to Colletti, could think of no better way out of this impasse than the slogan 'back to Kant'. Now, there is no doubt that, with the passage of time, some of the specific concepts or doctrines propounded in these pages may be found to be problematic, or untrue to any authentic Marxism, in ways now hidden from their authors. What is distinctive in these essays, though, is their attempt to think through a Marxist philosophy in which Marxism is neither collapsed into a variety of positivism, nor into a version of idealism, nor is reduced to a footnote to *The Critique of Pure Reason*. Whatever historically limited validity and specific set of doctrines or ideas herein propounded may possess, these essays are important in a much less limited way for the authentic Marxism towards which they attempt to move. They try to wed Marxism to no current intellectual fashion. They do not say that Marxism is 'really' Hegelian, or Kantian, or Aristotelian, or structuralist, or humanist. Marxism is distinctive and these essays are distinctive just insofar as they attempt to characterize that distinctiveness. In most of the essays, empiricism is the main enemy, but this anti-empiricism is based on a serious examination of ontological questions which is rooted in different categories from the currently fashionable anti-empiricist Marxism of Althusser, or Colletti or Timpanaro. There is an insistence that the problems of defining dialectical materialist thought and method can only be undertaken seriously by an examination of the ontological categories of physical necessity and *via* an elimination of the empiricist notion of causality.

A related common theme is the insistence on the need for a re-emphasis of the importance of materialism and on the necessity for a realist theory of science. It is apparent that the work of Roy Bhaskar (*A Realist Theory of Science*, Leeds 1975, *Hassocks* 1978) has been very influential in this area of discussion and we hope that one of the effects that these books might have is to encourage the development of Marxist philosophy in directions which his work, as well as recent books by Ted Benton (*Philosophical Foundations of the Three Sociologies*,

London 1977) and Russell Keat and John Urry (*Social Theory as Science*, *London* 1975), have opened up. In both these first two common lines of development, there is also a realist insistence on the part of many of the authors on how absolutely crucial it is to distinguish between ontology and epistemology. So much of the confusion and the unacceptable philosophical implications of recent British Althusserian writing can be traced back to the absence of this distinction, or to the inadequacy with which it is worked through. Indeed, some of that writing is naive enough to pose the explicit abandonment of epistemology, or ontology, or both. Many of the essays in these volumes single out the work of what we might call the British post-Althusserian idealists (especially Hindess and Hirst) as targets for attack, for their work is regarded as at one and the same time rather influential and philosophically extremely confused. In this sense, these volumes can be seen as an attempt to intervene in the general Marxist philosophical culture, especially of Britain and Australia, in an effort negatively to combat a specific, dominant, influential body of work and more positively to open up lines of research which we believe will prove much more useful.

Another feature of Marxist theoretical culture which requires critical attention is a certain common style of polemical writing. All too often, much of Marxist theoretical discussion has been marked by the method of 'impugning your opponent's credentials'. Frequently, the fixing of labels has replaced rational argument in these ongoing debates. Simply calling one's opponents 'idealist', 'positivist', 'empiricist', 'mechanical materialist', or 'Kantian', has apparently seemed to be all that is required in order to discredit their views. When all else fails, the accusation of failing to carry on the class struggle in philosophy (something allegedly done by those who do not accept the accuser's favourite version of Marxism) proves to be a sure winner. Much of the responsibility for this style of argument can be attributed to those Marxist philosophers whose work is insufficiently flexible and undogmatic. Indeed, it is the inflexibility and lack of openness of their views at any one time which leads to the subsequent recantations and auto-critiques rather than the organic growth and development of their positions. Whether intentionally or not, this gives rise to little bands of disciples whose function is to memorise slogans as answers to questions of which they in fact have very little understanding. In the hands of such people, Marxist philosophy has seemed closed rather than open, rigid rather than alive and changing. Among such disciples, especially those of British Althusserianism, abstract, critical thought has often been replaced by complicated technical jargon, whose effect has been numbing rather than the stimulation of clear, precise argument, free from inflexibility, rigidity, and dogmatism. Pat phrases and well-rehearsed slogans have prevailed; repetition and textual exegesis have become the hallmarks of a tradition no longer alive because no longer critical of itself. Each disciple followed his master in every new twist and turn from Marxism and back again, through every period of auto-critique. One could even learn slogans to explain why previous slogans were now to be considered erroneous. Without ceasing to be polemical in the best sense, these present essays are attempts at rational, argumentative, critical thought; they attempt to arrive at justified and well-supported conclusions by the method of Marx and Engels themselves, the method of critical analysis and argument, open to the possibilities of its own fallibility and limitations. In brief, these essays display that undogmatic and flexible character that has always characterized Marxist thinking at its best.

Two more remarks seem in order in this general introduction to these volumes. First, we hope that they will be read not only by philosophers but also by the many Marxists and non-Marxists who are troubled by the questions that are dealt with here. For example, many economists, engaged in difficult discussions about the concept of value and its status, have sensed the need for philosophical literature on the underlying problems of dialectical method and the theory of science. Many biologists and psychologists find that questions about the *materiality* of the objects of their study are directly raised by their own scientific work, and we hope that they will find the essays on materialism helpful. In general, questions of a philosophical character are raised from within very many kinds of intellectual work and practice, and we hope that the majority of these essays will be of use outside the boundaries of academic philosophy departments. Moreover, since in the English-speaking world at least, dominant modes of thought tend to be empiricist and pragmatic in character, we hope that these essays will link up with an alternative theoretical tradition, available to the workers' movement, which already exists in some areas of intellectual work other than philosophy, which speaks in the voices and accents of the cultural environment of that movement, and upon which that movement might draw in its struggle against capital. Hence, here as always, Marxist philosophy is a philosophy which is itself a political practice.

Secondly, it should already be clear from what we have said that the message of these volumes is not a triumphalist one: we do not believe that the authors have produced definitive solutions to the questions they discuss. These are not books of doctrines in search of disciples. Not only are there substantial differences of opinion among the various authors, but there is also in most of the essays a general tentativeness of tone, by and large a sense of modesty about what has been achieved, and an agreement on the need to recognize the fact that Marxist philosophy, in spite of its age, is still very far from having established even the outlines of a settled and confident adult form on many major issues.

JOHN MEPHAM

DAVID-HILLEL RUBEN

Introduction to the First Volume

THE importance for Marxists of coming to an understanding of the nature of dialectics and dialectical method is beyond controversy. One can identify, almost uncontroversially, specific examples of such dialectical thought and inquiry. The difficulties arise when we attempt to *say* what it is about such writing that makes it dialectical, and very little that is very illuminating has been said about this problem. Wildly general and ambitious slogans have usually replaced serious work. Scott Meikle refers, in his paper, to the 'pretence of galloping before one has yet shown the ability to walk'. Moreover, the nexus of issues that make up the problem of dialectics has suffered dual burial under the endless stream of Stalinist and neo-Stalinist diamat, and under the rather better-intentioned idealist and humanist reaction to that sort of quasi-positivist dogma.

What characterizes almost all of this previous writing on dialectics, and distinguishes it from the essays in this volume, is a failure to trace back the question of dialectics to the fundamental ontological issues which underlay that question. The diamat-inspired approach adopted a basically uncritical positivist ontology, weirdly and similarly uncritically admixed with half-understood Hegelian phrases. The humanist-idealist reaction, also uncritical of its own implicit ontological commitments, saw dialectics, like so much else, as the hallmark of human activity and hence confined its realm to society rather than all of nature. More recently, Lucio Colletti, whose work is critically examined in several of the essays in this volume, has argued that dialectics and materialism are necessarily incompatible, on the sole ground that they are so treated by Hegel. Colletti, like his predecessors in the debate on dialectics, allows assertion to replace a careful examination of ontological issues.

What most of these essays have in common is the belief

I

that the nature of dialectics and dialectical method can only be uncovered by an investigation of the realist ontological categories (many but by no means all of which derive from the influence of Aristotle) with which Marx worked and which informed his writing. The essays by Scott Meikle, Milton Fisk, and David-Hillel Ruben are all concerned, in very different ways, to elucidate various notions taken from the dialectical vocabulary by using categories such as real essence, nature, complexity, natural necessity, form, and development. These essays collectively pose the thesis that the dialectic can only be understood through a rejection of certain ontological categories and conceptions which find their home in positivist and empiricist modes of thought. Although the essays of Fisk and Ruben are also concerned with distinguishing the Marxist dialectic from an idealist dialectic, it is the essays by Chris Arthur and John Mepham which are centrally concerned with the task of differentiating Marxist method from Hegelian methodology, by means of a contrast between scientific or materialist and speculative or metaphysical methods of inquiry. What emerges, then, from the five essays is an attempt to reconstruct an authentic Marxist dialectic using non-positivist ontological categories which, at the same time, are not idealist in character. We might call such non-positivist, non-idealist ontological categories 'realist'.

Meikle carefully distinguishes dialectics from formal logic, and weds dialectics to the real essences or natures of things. Dialectics, according to Meikle, is concerned with grasping a whole in motion and uncovering the contradictions that constitute the moving principle of its development, and Meikle explains and deepens this idea both by examples drawn from *Capital*, as well as by an examination of the recent philosophical literature on such topics as necessity, essence, form, final causality, and potentiality. Meikle convincingly shows how, in the recent debate between Edgley and Colletti on Contradiction, both writers similarly conflate Dialectical with Logical Contradiction.

Milton Fisk begins his paper with the query: 'Is the dialectician, perhaps, coming from a completely different ontological standpoint?', and his reply is that 'dialectic is characterized by an ontology comprehensible only in a tradition that analysts and their forebears rejected long ago'. Fisk explains this ontology by the idea that entities are complex (not atomistic) and that every entity has essential to it a contradiction which is the source of its change. Fisk locates the contradictoriness of things in the fact that they are a combination of unity and diversity, that each thing is both a unit and *of* a certain kind, a combination which is unstable because of the tension it involves, and which is the foundation for more specific kinds of contradiction. Fisk concludes by undercutting the argument against the possibility of a materialist dialectic by arguing that atomism itself presupposes a form of idealism.

Ontological themes are again paramount in the paper by David-Hillel Ruben. Ruben argues that the content of the dialectic can be in part set out using the ideas of physical or natural necessity, developmental tendencies, and essence. He argues that Marx meant no more than what can be expressed by those terms in his use of dialectical terminology, and examines the *Introduction to the Grundrisse* to demonstrate this claim with reference to Marx's employment of the idea of concrete identity. Ruben then offers a philosophical defence of the idea of natural necessity, claming it as a distinctive sort of necessity from logical necessity, and finally shows how Marx's use of natural necessity differs from the empiricist accounts of causation and explanation, and what consequences those differences have for a Marxist conception of science.

C.A. Arthur's paper addresses itself to the ways in which Marx's dialectical methodology, although bearing some superficial resemblances to Hegel's, is itself not speculative and, on the contrary, is 'firmly grounded in material reality and is not open to the objections Marx himself propounded against philosophical speculation'. For Arthur, this task centres around showing how Marx's categories of abstract and concrete labour differ from the Hegelian notions of abstract and concrete universality. Through the use of these specifically Marxist categories of abstract and concrete, Arthur explains the content of Marx's critique of political economy, and specifically the nature of the contrast between the labour processes of a capitalist economy and of one governed by socialist planning. Through his critical concept of commodity fetishism, Marx criticises 'the estrangement of the abstract from the concrete in commodity production. He seeks the supersession of the contradiction, not in a speculative reconciliation, but in an historical change . . .'

Finally, in John Mepham's essay, the differences between Marx's and Hegel's method is again the central focus. Mepham uses the opportunity to criticize Rosdolsky's *The Making of Marx's 'Capital'* as an occasion to raise some very important questions of method. Perhaps in part as a reaction to his intellectual environment, Rosdolsky wished to stress the continuity between Hegel and Marx, between the *Grundrisse* and *Capital*, between philosophy and science. For Mepham, 'there is a profound difference between speculative or metaphysical discourse and the discourse of the sciences' and it is where Rosdolsky found continuities that Mepham seeks discontinuities, disanalogies, dissimilarities. Mepham illustrates this in detail by examining parallel passages in the *Grundrisse* and *Capital* and different passages from *Capital* itself which suggest two different methods of inquiry which Marx may have been following. In this way, both Arthur and Mepham are concerned to bring out the differences between philosophical or speculative method on the one hand and scientific method on the other, 'two different discourses' in Mepham's words, and Mepham concludes that 'In this, as in so many other instances, the making of Marx's *Capital* is possible only on condition that Hegel's methods are abandoned.'

1 *Dialectical Contradiction and Necessity*
SCOTT MEIKLE

I

THERE has long been a tendency among Marxists to speak disparagingly of formal logic. Some have gone beyond disparagement to outright rejection; formal logic has to be cast aside to make way for a 'higher' form of logic – dialectical logic. Others are prepared to admit formal logic, but only as a low-level enterprise compared to the 'higher' logic of dialectics, and conceive the relation between the two as comparable with the contrast sometimes drawn between 'higher' and 'lower' mathematics.[1]

The attitude to be adopted to formal logic is more than an isolated, technical question of Marxist philosophy. It is one way of approaching the question of what dialectics itself is. Dialectics, apart from being the last resort of the scoundrel, has been seen in many ways: (1) as a 'higher' form of logic, either replacing, or going beyond, formal logic; (2) as a method of analysis adequate for any content, whether sociology, history and political economy, or physics, biology, astronomy etc.; (3) as a method of exposition of a science; (4) as a method for the derivation of categories from a specific concrete content or subject-matter for the adequate theorization of that content; (5) as a 'philosophy', *Weltanschauung* or general conception of the world; (6) as not any sort of inner movement of the mind, but something mind-independent that exists in the realm of Being and imposes itself on the mind. Not all these things are uncontroversial or, on the face of it, consistent. To show them to be consistent and true, if they are, needs a lot of work that has yet to be done. Authors who want to assert all these things at once, like Henri Lefebvre,[2] do not help matters by side-stepping that work with reassuring formulae to the effect that the

5

dialectic is many apparently incompatible things at once which can only be integrated into 'an open totality perpetually in the process of being transcended.'[3] This is a pretence at galloping before one has yet shown the ability to walk. With the present level of comprehension of Marx's dialectic, distorted as it is by all the forces that have formed, misformed and divided the international working-class movement particularly over the last half-century, it would be more suitable to set oneself the aim of learning to crawl.

II

Volume I of *Capital* represents Marx's most systematic application of his conception of dialectic. The question may usefully be asked, therefore, whether in that work Marx dispenses with formal logic or not. The answer is that he did not. He criticizes constantly the illicit assumptions, confusions and false inferences by which authors with whom he disagrees arrive at their conclusions. Certainly his disagreements with them are based ultimately on the irreconcilability of their views with his own, and his own views are inseparably tied to, and could not be attained without, his dialectical method. But this fact does not impart a dialectical character to his arguments against those opposed positions, nor does it imply that Marx's criticisms amount to saying that in every case what is wrong with those positions is that they are undialectical. Marx sees both logic and illogic in the works of classical political economy; a quite separate question is that he considered classical political economy as a whole to be inadequate because its 'analytical method', as he calls it, is unhistorical and for that reason, in part, undialectical. Two brief and random examples must suffice.

First: Marx observes that 'the process of exchange gives to the commodity which it has converted into money not its value but its specific value-form. Confusion between these two attributes has misled some writers into maintaining that the value of gold and silver is imaginary.'[4] In the accompanying footnote he points out that not all authors have been confused in this way. Galiani, for example, had held that,

'Gold and silver have value as metals before they are money.' Whereas Locke had held that, 'The universal consent of mankind gave to silver on account of its qualities which made it suitable for money, an imaginary value.'

Second: in 'Senior's "Last Hour"' Marx shows Professor W. Nassau Senior's error to lie in his failure to comprehend that the value of raw materials etc., is transmitted automatically and pro-rata to the finished product whatever the duration of the working-period. Though Marx chooses to aim his attack at that error of 'analysis' on Senior's part, it is clearly implicit that he is criticizing Senior for committing a *non-sequitur*. Given Senior's assumptions (1) that in the course of a year the manufacturer with a starting capital of £100,000 and a one-year turnover period, produces goods worth £115,000, and (2) that the total annual return recovers his capital outlay with a gross profit of 15 percent, it does not follow, (3) that each working day can be divided into a period in which part of the capital is reproduced and another period in which part of the annual profit is produced. One could equally conclude that each hour, second or microsecond was divided into two such periods.

Errors of this kind do not of themselves involve dialectics, and recourse to dialectics is not required for their exposure. It is useful to contrast with them an error that does involve dialectics. Such an error is committed by Böhm-Bawerk where, in *Karl Marx and the Close of his System*, he tries to locate 'the error in the Marxist system'. Böhm-Bawerk, failing to understand that central to Marx's (dialectical) method was the derivation of categories from *specific* concrete contents or subject-matters, could see no reason why Marx should make labour the starting point of *Capital* rather than utility, and concludes that the choice was arbitrary and without justification. The source of Böhm-Bawerk's incomprehension lies in the method he employs in developing his argument. His straightforward and unsupplemented application of formal logic is incapable on its own of establishing any categorical difference between labour and utility which it can only regard indifferently as mere terms to substitute for variables in argument-forms. But the asymmetry in Marx's treatment of labour and utility derives from the different *real natures* of labour and utility; the distinction lies in an *essential* difference and hence is anything but arbitrary. Böhm-Bawerk's characteristic empiricist way of employing formal logic does not typically incline towards the study of the real essences of the items denoted by the terms, and he finds it possible in consequence

> to conclude that the abstraction from particular use-value to use-value in general is just as acceptable, in principle, as the abstraction from concrete to abstract labour; and that, therefore, on strictly logical grounds there is nothing to choose between the two 'models', one of which takes embodied labour as the common property of commodities and therefore the basis of value, and the other of which casts the function of commodities of satisfying needs in this role.[5]

The failure of Böhm-Bawerk's criticisms has its source in his failure to understand both formal logic and dialectics, and the relation between them.

Such misunderstandings have the major part of their basis in a false philosophy of logic; that is, ultimately, in a false set of metaphysical, ontological and epistemological assumptions that accompany a false conception of logic, and of its role in the cognitive process. It would, however, be an oversimplification to suggest that the errors exist only at the level of philosophical logic. Logic, the philosophy of logic and the application of logic do not exist in mutually independent forms. The interconnections are found, not only in the attitudes adopted towards the analysis of essences, but also in those adopted towards time, change and development. To the extent that one operates exclusively with ordinary formal logic as it exists, and it exists in a form that centrally builds around timeless, untensed propositions, attention will be directed away from questions of time and change. The form in which ordinary formal logic exists cannot easily be separated from a certain static view of the world and an idealist metaphysics and ontology. The distinction may be made theoretically, but in practice the two are connected. Formal logic exists in the form that it does partly because of the metaphysical and ontological (pre-) dispositions of its practitioners. This was the case in Hegel's time, when the formal logic of the day was a debased Aristotelian syllogistic, the accompanying world-view a static one allied to a classificatory conception of knowledge based on definition *per genus ad differentiam*, and the whole lot interlocked in a philosophical-ideological unity. The same sort of relationships hold at the present time, though the items so related may have changed somewhat. Thus, though in principle formal logic alone need not incline a thinker like Böhm-Bawerk towards *a priorism*, in practice it easily can. This is to scratch only the surface of the issues involved; one could add one further scratch in noting that Marxist authors have repeatedly railed, as Hegel did, against abstract identity $(A = A)$, usually with scant achievement. Few have come as near to the heart of the problem as Trotsky did with his terse observation about time: 'everything exists in time; and existence itself is an uninterrupted process of transformation; time in consequence is a fundamental element of existence. Thus the axiom "A" is equal to "A", signifies that a thing is equal to itself if it does not change, that is, if it does not exist.'[6]

III

Marx did not conceive dialectics to be a 'higher' form of logic, either replacing, or standing above, formal logic. This can be seen from Marx's own writings. In 1857-8 Marx was writing the *Grundrisse*. It consists of seven notebooks, of which the first, dated July 1857, was the unfinished section on Bastiat, and which has the form of an introduction.[7] What finally appeared as the celebrated 'Introduction,' however, was a notebook quite separate from the rest of the series, and it is characterized both by its employment of Hegelian terms and by its concentration on general questions of method. It marks an important departure from Marx's previous writings on political economy. So much is familiar. What produced this departure is also familiar: it was Marx's re-reading of Hegel, and in particular his re-reading of the *Logic*, which he announced at the time with the joy of discovery in a letter to Engels.[8]

The question is: what was it that Marx had rediscovered in

Hegel in the winter of 1857–8? It is insufficient to answer that he had rediscovered dialectics; what we want to know is what this means. (I shall not engage in the question of how much Marx owes directly or indirectly to Hegel. I shall suggest later that some of Marx's most fundamental conceptions are Aristotelian in character. It is for scholars to unearth whether Marx drew them from Hegel alone, from Aristotle through Hegel, directly from Aristotle, or in whatever other ways are conceivable). Perhaps one goes some way towards an answer with Martin Nicolaus's conclusion that 'for Marx, as for Hegel, the problem of grasping a thing' had become 'firstly the problem of grasping that it is in motion'.[9] Or more specifically: 'If the society as a whole is to be grasped in motion, in process, it is first and foremost essential to comprehend the dynamics of the direct production process, because – as Hegel said – the energy, the drive of the whole has its source in the underlying contradiction.'[10] But this is still too unspecific, because it is consistent with different views of what dialectics is. It is consistent with the *diamat* interpretation according to which dialectics is 'a logic in the sense that it describes the necessary laws of things at the most general level, and thus gives a method of thinking about the world which is of universal application'.[11] It is equally consistent with the view that dialectics is not a *logic* at all, and that there is no general method of universal application.

Marx's ideas on the matter are made quite clear in another letter to Engels written only a fortnight after the one cited above. In criticizing Lassalle's Hegelian pretensions he writes: 'He will learn to his cost, that it is one thing to develop a science to the point where one can present it dialectically, and something else altogether to apply an abstract and ready-made system of logic.'[12] It is quite clear that Marx is rejecting, on his own part, any idea of dialectics as anything we would recognize as a *system of logic*, and that he is rejecting as incompatible with scientific method the idea that there is any ready-made system lying around which will, in virtue of its 'universal applicability', if applied to any sphere of phenomena, thereby beget its scientific and critical comprehension.

This letter of Marx's introduces another consideration, again a familiar one, that Marx's dialectical method requires that the categories in which a science is presented dialectically be derived from a detailed appropriation of the concrete empirical data of the field in question. The science has, as he indicated, to be developed up to a certain point before it is susceptible of dialectical presentation; one cannot begin with the dialectical presentation. The point is made again in the *Grundrisse*:

> The concrete is concrete because it is the concentration of many determinations, hence unity in the diverse. It appears in the process of thinking, therefore, as a process of concentration, as a result, not as a point of departure, even though it is the point of departure in reality and hence also the point of departure for observation and conception.[13]

This passage helps illuminate a methodological error commonly found in certain schools of Marxist thought, and spotlights their dogmatic and sometimes politically apologetic character. The 'concrete' figures twice in this passage. Its first occurrence, as the *result* of scientific enquiry, is familiar in Marxist literature, and is often made the focus of a supposed major methodological difference with empiricism which is supposed to regard the 'concrete' only as 'the given' or empirical raw material for science. The second occurrence of the 'concrete' in this quote, however, is often overlooked though it has a fundamental importance. Abstractions and categories do not arrive from nowhere; they have to be constructed. They have to be constructed through a process of appropriating the concrete empirical data of the area under investigation ('the point of departure for observation and conception'), of critical appraisal of the ordinary concepts (and the preliminary abstractions) in which the data may be described or interpreted and of 'concept formation'. This aspect of Marx's conception of scientific practice, this movement from 'concrete' to abstraction, is overlooked by those Marxists who find a superficial methodological difference with empiricism, and a characterization of Marx's method that is little short of parody, in seeing empiricist method as a movement from concrete to abstract and then portraying Marxist method as *a simple reversal* of this: a movement from abstract to concrete. Such Marxists leave themselves with nowhere to get their abstractions from, except perhaps thin-air, talmudism or political expediency; but at all events not from the reality under investigation. (If there is any particular field that illustrates this misconception better than any other it is the field of analysis of the nature of the Soviet Union. Here this methodological over-simplification can often be seen, in its origins and nature, to be less of a disinterested 'theoretical' confusion than the basis of a rationale for, or consequence of (or both), the pragmatic political requirements of some post-revolutionary nation State.)

The categories and abstractions of a dialectical presentation are specific to the particular area of reality that is under study. There can, therefore, be no dialectical system that is of universal application. The idea of a general scheme independent of specific content, that is of specific areas of study or specific 'wholes' or 'totalities', is therefore a nonsense in Marx's terms.

As to the idea that such a general system would take the form of a dialectical *logic*, one has to be clear about what a logical system is. The generality of a system lies in its being divested of specific content. The generality of a system of logic lies in its being totally divested of any content whatever, that is in its being formal. Hegel makes the point[14], when he observes that the starting point of logic resides in Aristotle's achievement, namely: to come to grips with thought in a systematic way by extracting its common forms from their myriad of daily contexts of use and application where they are submerged beneath the actual contents being discussed, and making those forms themselves objects of awareness and study. Of its nature, this step requires the total separation of form from content, so that form and content become contrasted and opposed. Hegel himself goes on to argue that the development of knowledge requires the development of new thought-forms (*denkformen*), and that consequently the finished and completed nature of

Aristotelian logic indicates its limited nature and the necessity for advancing knowledge of moving over and beyond it. This latter movement he conceived in terms of the attainment of a higher conception of thought in which form and content are re-united. Now it may be possible, in the case of Hegel's idealism, for this re-unification to take the form of a 'higher' logic that is formalizable – the point will not be argued here, though it should be noted that at least one author has thought this possible and tried to achieve the formalization.[15] But such a formalization is certainly not possible *a priori* for Marx's conception of dialectic, because 'content' for Marx signifies a class of specific 'wholes', or fields of reality to be studied, not a single general category. The categories with which a particular area of reality is to be grasped dialectically are the result of the analysis of the real natures or essences of the items that inhabit that area. Whether those categories are capable of application to other areas is, then, for Marx, an empirical question that turns on the real natures concerned. Logic can be formalized precisely because abstract form is separated from content and represented alone in the abstract. It is clear that no such formalization is *a priori* possible for Marx's dialectic, and from that it follows that dialectic in Marx's conception is not a logic. (It may, perhaps, be made such *a posteriori*, but the condition to be satisfied for the attainment of the level of generalization that would be required would be that we had come to know everything about everything.) To think of dialectic as a general scheme independent of specific content is, in Marx's terms, either a nonsense or a cheque drawn on the future development of human cognition that may, for all we know now, bounce. The attempt to undermine a 'bourgeois critique of dialectic as logic' such as Popper's[16], by means of a reshaped 'conception of logic different from that of formal logic' in which there is a *general* fusion of logic and ontology, where 'logic must become ontologic' as proposed by Roy Edgley[17], is therefore unnecessary. The bourgeois critique of dialectic as logic, and any Marxist attempt to rebut such a critique in the way proposed, are alike based on one and the same misconception of what dialectic is in the hands of Marx.

In what follows I shall be concerned with questions about

the nature of dialectic and not much with formal logic.
However, having suggested that formal logic (in some form,
possibly tensed) and dialectics can co-exist, the matter cannot be left without saying something, however perfunctory,
about the relation between formal logic and dialectic. The
most promising view seems to be the one sketched by Trotsky,
that dialectic concerns 'our thinking insofar as it is not
limited to the daily problems of life but attempts to arrive
at an understanding of more complicated and drawn-out
processes.' 'Dialectics does not deny the syllogism', but its
importance is for higher theoretical tasks while that of 'the
simple syllogism (is) for more elementary tasks'[18]. Dialectics
is not a 'higher' form of logic, but (as will be argued below)
a higher form of method (possibly applicable only in social
science) within which ordinary logic is transformed by being
assigned a definite sphere of operation and efficacy.

V

The conclusion that formal logic can coexist with dialectics is
only negative: dialectics is *not* a replacement for, or a higher
form of, formal logic; it is not a 'ready-made' system awaiting
application to produce a science. What, then, is it? Marx's
comments on Lassalle are consistent with the possibility
that other sciences could be brought to the point of dialectical
presentation. Is dialectic, then, simply a method of ex-
pounding, or presenting results? Clearly not. Marx considered Darwin to have given biology a dialectical form,
even though he described to Engels Darwin's presentation as
'grossly unfolded in the English manner'[19], and complained
to Lassalle that 'one has to put up with the gross English
mode of development, of course'.[20]

It seems safe to assume that there is sufficient agreement
among Marxists that, paraphrasing Nicolaus, Marx's dialectic has all to do with grasping a whole in motion, and uncovering the contradiction that constitutes the moving
principle of its development. The question now is: what does
this mean? (1) What is a 'whole' and how is such a thing
identified; (2) what is a 'contradiction'; (3) how does a

contradiction supply motive power for a development?

These questions may be approached by looking at the development of *Capital* Volume I, and especially Part I 'Commodities and Money', comprising chapters 1 to 3, 'The Commodity', 'The Process of Exchange', and 'Money, or the Circulation of Commodities'. Why did Marx begin *Capital* with the commodity? Certainly not because it was the *obvious* starting point, though it might seem to be so now. Nor because, as Marx puts it in the first sentence of the book, 'the wealth of societies in which the capitalist mode of production prevails appears as an "immense collection of commodities"; the individual commodity appears as its elementary form'. Despite Marx's suggestion in the ensuing sentence that this *is* the reason for beginning where he does ('Our investigation *therefore* begins with the analysis of the commodity.' – italics added), it clearly is not the real reason. Marx begins with the commodity, but not because it is the obvious concrete reality, 'the point of departure for observation and conception'.[21] On the contrary, his beginning with it presupposes the results of his entire analysis. Recall Marx's observation that a science must be developed up to a certain point before it is capable of dialectical presentation; the final section will note Marx's recognition that the scientific results of classical political economy, flawed though its 'analytical method' may be, provide the basis that makes possible the developed critical-science *(Kritik der Wissenschaft)*. It should hardly be a surprise that his choice of starting point should presuppose the results of his analysis. Marx's analysis of the commodity, as it unfolds the phases of transition that the value-form passes through, reveals it to be that 'concrete' which 'appears in the process of thinking . . . as a result, not as a point of departure', and not to be that other unanalyzed 'concrete' which *is* 'the point of departure for observation and conception'.[22] As he explains in a familiar passage, the method of enquiry 'has to appropriate the material in detail, to analyse its different forms of development and to track down their inner connexion. Only after this work has been done can the real movement be appropriately presented'.[23] The commodity-form is made the point of departure in 'the method of presentation', because the enquiry had revealed it to be the source of 'the life of the subject matter', of 'the laws of motion' of the organism.[24]

This can be approached in another way. Why, for example did Marx not begin with money? Because, as he says, 'The only difficulty in the concept of the money form is that of grasping the universal equivalent form, and hence the general form of value as such'. But this difficulty can be overcome, he continues, 'by working backwards to . . . the expanded form of value, and its constitutive element is . . . x commodity A = y commodity B. The simple commodity-form is, therefore, the germ of the money form'.[25] Hence Marx begins with the commodity in its most primitive form: 'The Simple, Isolated, or Accidental Form of Value.'

All the contradictions of capitalist commodity-production have at their heart the contradiction between use-value and exchange-value. Marx reveals this contradiction to lie at the heart of the commodity-form as such, even in its simplest and most primitive form. The commodity-form of the product of labour appears, then, as pregnant with certain potentialities or lines of development which may be realized given the right historical conditions.

The *simple* form of value itself contains the polar opposition between, and the union of, use-value and exchange-value. At the very beginning of his analysis of the development of the value-form (which, he explicitly says, coincides with the development of the commodity-form[26]) he writes: 'The whole mystery of the form of value lies hidden in this simple form. Our real difficulty, therefore, is to analyze it.' He continues with two observations. First that 'the relative form of value and the equivalent form are two inseparable moments, which belong to and mutually condition each other'. Secondly: 'but at the same time they are mutually exclusive and opposed extremes'. Concerning the first, he observes that the value of linen cannot be expressed in linen; 20 yards of linen = 20 yards of linen is not an expression of value. 'The value of the linen can therefore only be expressed relatively, that is in another commodity. The relative form of value of the linen therefore presupposes that some other commodity confronts it in the equivalent form.' Concerning the second: 'on the other hand, this other

commodity which figures as the equivalent, cannot simultaneously be in the relative form of value ... The same
commodity cannot, therefore, simultaneously appear in both
forms in the same expression of value. These forms rather
exclude each other as *polar opposites*.'[27]

This polar opposition within the simple form is an 'internal
opposition' which as yet remains *hidden within* the individual
commodity in its simple form: 'The internal opposition
between use-value and exchange-value, hidden within the
commodity, is therefore represented on the surface by an
external opposition,'[28] that is the relation between *two*
commodities such that one (the equivalent form) counts only
as a use-value, while the other (the relative form) counts only
as an exchange-value. 'Hence the simple form of value of the
commodity is the simple form of the opposition between use-
value and value which is contained in the commodity.'[29]

Yet, what Marx finds in the *simple* form of value is not only
the key to *understanding* the money form, but also the impel-
ling force that *begets* it, or in his metaphor, the germ from
which it germinates. For he argues that the simple form is
'insufficient', and if there is to be historical development
(of the value-form), then it must, as a matter of *necessity*,
be development towards the money-form. 'We perceive
straight away the insufficiency of the simple form of value: it
is an embryonic form which must undergo a series
of metamorphoses before it can ripen into the price form.'[30]
Looking at it from the farther end of the development,
'Money necessarily crystallizes out of the process of exchange,
in which different products of labour are in fact equated with
each other and thus converted into commodities.' The
historical development, the deepening and broadening of
exchange activity between people that goes along with the
development of private labour in production relations,
develops the opposition between use-value and exchange-
value, and begets a need, a necessity, for a fuller commercial
expression, that is there is a *drive*, arising from the 'insufficiency' of the simple form, towards 'an independent form
of value', money. 'At the same rate, then, as the transformation of the products of labour into commodities is accomplished, one particular commodity is transformed into

money.'[31] (The process is not a unilinear progression of forms, of course, but a more complex process in which forms overlap, interpenetrate and develop each other). The development, therefore, is a necessary one arising from the 'internal opposition' inherent in the commodity-form of the product, and from the 'insufficiency' of its simple form. This insufficiency is rectified by daily practice and ingenuity; by a series of 'easy transitions' the more developed value-form is attained. ('But only the action of society can turn a particular commodity into the universal equivalent'[32]).

There is no incompatability between seeing the historical movement as one of forms on the one hand, and as one of social relations of production on the other. Thus, to see the drive of development in the 'insufficiency' of the simple form of value, is not an alternative to seeing it as lying in the social relations of production. 'Insufficiency' is a two-place predicate. Something has to be insufficient for something else. The simple form of value is insufficient for the developing social relations of private production, that is, for the progressive transformation of the products of labour into commodities and subjects of exchange.

The attainment of the developed money-form creates enough room for the antagonism immanent in the simple commodity or value-form to move; the germ germinates. Further on in *Capital*, Marx, referring back to the discussion of the polar antagonism inherent in the simple commodity-form, writes: 'We saw in a former chapter that the exchange of commodities implies contradictory and mutually exclusive conditions. The further development of the commodity does not abolish these contradictions, but rather provides the form within which they have room to move.'[33] And in turn, the further development of the money-form itself begets new latent oppositions that can in the right conditions burst forth into 'absolute contradictions'. Thus, for example, when money develops beyond its function of means of circulation into a means of payment, there is a new 'contradiction immanent in the function of money as a means of payment'.

> This contradiction bursts forth in that aspect of a commercial and industrial crisis which is known as a monetary crisis . . . money

suddenly and immediately changes over from its merely nominal shape, money on account, into hard cash. Profane commodities can no longer replace it, the use-value of commodities becomes valueless, and their value vanishes in the face of their own form of value ... In a crisis, the antithesis between commodities and their value-form, money, is raised to the level of an absolute contradiction.[34]

VI

Some questions about Marx's conception of contradiction may now be confronted. Colletti has posed the questions: is a dialectical contradiction a *logical* contradiction (that is a breach of the law of non-contradiction in formal logic) existing in reality?; is it a *non-logical* contradiction (that is a 'real opposition') existing in reality?; or is it a logical contradiction (non)existing in an unreal 'reality'.[35] Of the three alternatives he adopts the obviously absurd one, namely the last. He arrives at it because he takes the views: (1) that formal logical contradictions cannot exist in the real world, and (2) that dialectical contradiction has to be logical contradiction. With impeccable consistency he proceeds into the wilderness with the inference that since dialectical contradiction does characterize capitalist society, then capitalist society does not exist. (Or, as he puts it, capitalist society cannot be real, and can only be an 'unreal' reality. This original conception is given plausibility by an ingenious recourse to the theory of alienation which need not detain us.) Edgley, in reply, rightly insists on 'the fact that capitalism seems to be only too bloody real',[36] and that therefore its contradictions must exist as features of the real world. Then, facing up seriously to Marx's absolutely fundamental (Hegelian) idea that the two poles united in an opposition *necessitate* one another ('belong to and mutually condition each other'), Edgley seeks elucidation of the nature of the necessity involved by resort to logic and logical necessity; getting around the argument that logical relations are not features of the real world by saying that this is true only of bourgeois formal or truth-functional logical relations, and not of Marxist 'ontologic'. (What Edgley has done is to wrongly locate Colletti's error in Colletti's view (1), that formal logical contradictions cannot exist in the real world, while the error really lies in Colletti's second view (2) that dialectical contradiction is logical contradiction. This latter is a view that Edgely shares with Colletti, and he writes: 'Colletti is right to insist on the essentially logical character of contradiction, and thus of dialectic.'[37]) As already seen, however, the solution to the question of the nature of the necessity that unites opposites within an opposition in which each pole 'necessitates' the other, is not to be found in the direction of Edgley's fusion of ontology and logic in an Ontologic. One is stuck with formal logic and dialectics. So the problem is this: what sort of necessity is in question here?

It is apparent from some recent Marxist work, that there is a tendency to construe the necessity as 'logical necessity'. What sometimes underlies this is a tendency to elevate formal logic beyond the world of humanity. To counteract this it is salutory to recall Hegel's vividly suggestive onslaught on that very tendency in *The Science of Logic*. Recalling Aristotle's intriguing statement that 'this science ... seems to be a more than human possession'[38], Hegel writes:

> We do not indeed say of our feelings, impulses or interests that they serve us, rather do they count as independent forces and powers, so that to have this particular feeling, to desire and to will this particular thing and to be interested in it – just this, is what we are. But probably we are more conscious of obeying our feelings, impulses, passions, interests, not to mention habits, than of having them in our possession, still less, in view of our intimate union with them, of their being at our disposal. Such determinations of feeling and mind soon show themselves as *particular* in contrast to the *universality* which we are conscious ourselves of being and in which we have our freedom; and we are disposed to regard ourselves as caught up in these particular states and dominated by them.

The same, he suggests, goes for attitudes to 'forms of thought', for the quotation continues:

> Consequently it is much more difficult to believe that the forms of thought which permeate all our ideas – whether these are purely theoretical or contain a matter belonging to feeling, impulse, will – are means for us, rather than that we serve them, that in fact they

have us in their possession; what is there more in *us* as against them, how shall *we*, how shall *I*, set myself up as *more* universal than they, which are the universal as such?[39]

These passages are taken somewhat out of context, because Hegel's concern is to develop the contrast between the 'level of Understanding', and 'Reason' whose function is to surmount understanding, and outflank the contradictions it produces, by framing new categories and forms of thought that allow human cognition to proceed and facilitate deeper penetration into, and discoveries about, essences. (The passages are even more out of context in that I have cast them, deliberately, in a way that lends itself to a materialist interpretation by leaving out Hegel's idealist doctrine of Notion.) Nevertheless they may serve to make the point. A not so dissimilar view to Hegel's is taken by Quine, though expressed less graphically:

> Mathematics and logic, central as they are to the conceptual scheme, tend to be accorded such immunity (*sc.* from revision – S.M.), in view of our conservative preferences for revisions which disturb the system least; and herein, perhaps, lies the 'necessity' which the laws of mathematics and logic are felt to enjoy ... Logical laws ... because again of their crucial position ... are laws an apt revision of which might offer the most sweeping simplification of our whole system of knowledge. Thus the laws of mathematics and logic may, despite all 'necessity', be abrogated.[40]

Of course, one does not have to accept Quine's logical conventionalism, but the alternative accounts of what 'logical necessity' might be provide even less of a basis for understanding the necessity that unites opposites within an opposition. There are three possibilities, it would seem, for '*logical* necessity'. Either it does not exist; or it is conventional; or it exists but is indefinable. If it does not exist it cannot help with the problem, and likewise if it is conventional as will be seen. As to the third possibility, one can say nothing until a coherent case has been made for it. I reject the theology of Plantinga and Dummett who in seeking for something for man to be less than, think they find something of the kind in logic.

So 'logical necessity' does not promise to account for the necessity that unites opposites within a contradiction. The unity of use-value and exchange-value within the commodity is certainly *not* something which, despite all necessitation between the two poles, may be abrogated (on Quine's conventionalist account). Not, that is, without 'abrogating' the commodity itself; for the commodity is precisely the unity of use-value and exchange-value. Use-value can exist alone. But exchange-value cannot; it presupposes use-value because only what has use-value can have exchange-value. What has exchange-value, a commodity, is, thus, necessarily use-value and exchange-value brought into a unity. The commodity-form of the product of labour has *as its essence* the unity of the two. That is what it *is*. Their conjunction or unity constitutes its essence. (Such a formulation of its essence is unfinished and incomplete. Its full specification requires the analysis of exchange-value itself as the phenomenal form of value, whose substance, in turn, is abstract labour. This incompleteness, however, does not affect the present argument.) Use-value and exchange-value are, therefore, not 'merely' abstractions arrived at in thought about reality; they are constituents of reality in partaking in the essence of the commodity. And the opposition or contradiction between the two poles is a constituent of reality also, (although in the *simple* commodity or value-form it appears only primitively in the fact that the same commodity cannot act simultaneously as relative and as equivalent form of value).

The commodity *is* the unity of use-value and exchange-value, in precisely the same way that water *is* H_2O, that light *is* a stream of photons, or that gold *is* the element with the atomic number 79. All these statements are *necessarily* true. They state truths that are true of necessity, not in virtue of any logical or 'conceptual' connexions, but in virtue of the essences or real natures of the entities in question. Water is necessarily H_2O. Anything that is not H_2O cannot *be* water, however closely it may resemble water in appearance, and the 'cannot' is ontological not epistemic. To be H_2O is of the essence of water. We did not always know this, of course; it was a *discovery* people made about the essence of water (and one which may need to be recast if future theoretical development requires it). The real natures of entities do not lie around on the surface ready for our immediate appropriation. They have to be uncovered by investigation and thought. And to acquire such knowledge is what it is to know what things are and to understand them. Aristotle: 'There is epistemic knowledge of a thing only when we know its essence.'[41] These are necessary truths, and the necessity of their truth arises from essences (or aspects of them) that have been discovered. It might be that some philosophers who use the language of 'possible worlds' mean the same thing when they say that such truths are *logically* necessary' because they are 'true in all possible worlds'. If that is what is meant, then there may be no harm in the use of the expression 'logically necessary' to describe such truths. Though there may be harm in it if it suggests to anyone that 'logic' in some sense is the source of the necessity involved, rather than the real natures. Another danger in the use of the expression is that it may suggest that there is some difference, where there is none, between the necessity involved in the sort of identity statements we have been considering ('water is H_2O') and statements that we shall be considering which attribute some tendency or potentiality to an essence. There is no difference. The statement attributing a tendency to an essence is necessarily true for just the same reason that an identity statement may be, viz. that it arises from an essence. To see a difference between them, for example that the latter is 'logical' necessity whereas the former is 'natural' or 'physical' necessity, would be wrong. Of course, statements recording the *actualization* of an inherent tendency or the *realization* of a potentiality cannot be necessary truths, for the potentiality might (in some possible world) not be realized. That the development occurs, or that the tendency or potentiality is realized, is not necessary; though, if the development does occur, that it takes the sort of course it does is necessary. Thus, a statement like 'In all possible worlds (where the thing exists) its essence is XYZ' is necessarily true, and in the same sense of 'necessary truth' a statement like 'In all possible worlds (where the thing exists and its essence develops its potentialities) the development is of the form PQR' is necessarily true. An example would be: where the commodity form exists and develops, its development will pass from the simple form of value to the universal form.

There is no need to elaborate on this notion of necessary truth. A fuller account of it (though one not wholly hospitable to the view adopted here) is given by its modern expositor S. Kripke.[42] It should be noted, however, that defining 'necessary truth' as 'true in all possible worlds' need not be part of a view that necessary truths are true in virtue of essences. For if the proposition 'if p, then q' is 'logically necessary' if and only if in every possible world where p is true, q is true also, then the proposition could be true by coincidence (since it could be by mere chance that p and q are always true together) and still be 'logically necessary' in the sense defined. For the essentialist view of necessary truth adopted here, this is not enough. There will have to be some *essential* reason why p and q are so conjoined. It is in that sort of reason, and not in the formal satisfaction of 'logical necessity' as defined, that we can find the sort of basis that we need for the kind of necessity we are seeking. The main point is that such a conception of necessary truth explains the necessity that unites use-value and exchange-value as opposites within the commodity-form without having recourse either (a) to 'logical' necessity or 'conceptual' connections, with all the absurdities that crop up in trying to squeeze out a solution on that basis, or (b) to the conception of ontologic, with its unacceptable *general* fusion of ontology and logic over all domains. It is worth noting that such an account of necessity, an account of truths as necessary in virtue of real natures, is based upon a materialist separation of ontology from epistemology. The fundamental hallmark of much idealist philosophical thinking of the bourgeois epoch, from Descartes, through Berkeley and Hume, to Mach, Avenarius, Russell and recent logical empiricism, has been precisely the fusion of ontology into epistemology. It is at this fusion, or subordination, that Lenin aims much of his attack on Bogdanov and company in *Materialism and*

Emperio-Criticism. If Colletti and Edgley are wrong to see dialectical contradiction as essentially logical, then in Colletti's case it is strange that he should ever have come to such a view, because his own reliance on Kant for making the distinction between opposition that is 'either *logical*, in-involving contradiction *(durch den Widerspruch)*, or *real*, *i.e.* devoid of contradiction *(Ohne Widerspruch)*'[43], leads him into reproducing Kant's account of a real or non-logical opposition as:

> one in which the two predicates of a thing are opposed, but not through the principle of contradiction . . . Two forces, one imparting movement to a body in one direction, and the other imparting an equal effect in the opposite direction, do not contradict each other: they are both possible as predicates of a single body. The outcome is equilibrium, which is a thing *(repraesentabile)*. This is an instance of true opposition. In fact the effect of one of the two tendencies, were it acting in isolation, is negated by the other, and both these tendencies are true predicates of a single thing and are attached to it simultaneously.[44]

What is interesting about this is the resemblance it bears to one of Marx's few statements about contradiction:

> We saw in a former chapter that the exchange of commodities implies contradictory and mutually exclusive conditions. The further development of the commodity does not abolish these contradictions, but rather provides the form within which they have room to move. This is, in general, the way in which real contradictions are resolved. For instance, it is a contradiction to depict one body as constantly falling towards another and at the same time constantly flying away from it. The ellipse is a form of motion within which this contradiction is both realized and resolved.[45]

It could not be clearer that Marx's effective use of contradiction (barring pedantic distinctions, both Kant and Marx speak, not of *tendencies* to motion being imparted, but actual movements, so that the conjunction of the two statements attributing motions would really yield a formal contradiction) was that of real, not logical, opposition, and that consequently the mutual necessitation of the two poles in an opposition must involve a necessity other than logical.

VII

So far only that aspect of Marx's contradiction that concerns the relation of necessity that exists between the two poles united in it has been considered. There is another aspect which also involves necessity, and which the 'essential' necessity so far discussed is not, as it stands, adequate to account for. The idea of truths being necessary in virtue of essences has been developed by Kripke only in relation to particular entities (specifically, bearers of proper names, like Nixon or the planet Venus) or kinds of entity (natural kinds, like gold or water). Dialectic, however, is concerned with big systems of things and kinds; more than that, it is concerned with them in their organic process of development, change and reproduction. It is on this that the other aspect of dialectical contradiction has direct bearing.

The poles in an opposition are not just united. They also repel one another. They are brought together in a unity, but within that unity they are in tension. The real historical existence of the product of labour in the commodity-form provides an analogue of a centripetal force that contains the centrifugal forces of the mutual repulsion of use-value and exchange-value within it. But in its simple form, the commodity is an unstable equilibrium. It is pregnant with possibilities, which history may present either with the conditions for the realization of those possibilities, or with the indefinite variety of conditions that will frustrate their realization. Given the right conditions, the embryo will develop its potentiality; and the simple form of value will undergo the metamorphoses that take the commodity from its embryo, through infancy to early adolescence with the attainment of the universal form of value, money. This line of development is not accidental or fortuitous; it is not a process of aggregating contingent and extraneous additions. It is, rather, a process of development of the potentialities within, and the increasing differentiation of, an original whole. If history does not block the growth of exchange activity, then that growth will find out the inadequacy of the simple form of value. Then, looked at from the point of view of efficient causation, those engaged in that activity, being rational and inventive in the face of the problems thrown up by their developing class interests, will act so as to solve their practical difficulties by measures that overcome that insufficiency to the requirements of their developing commerce. The solution to their practical problems is the money-form. 'The desires which move in the development of institutions develop with those institutions.'[46] Not every move which in fact served to promote the money-form will have been made with that end in view. Nonetheless, that such moves did serve that end may explain why they did not lapse. Looked at from the point of view of final causation, money is the final cause of this phase of social development. This is not to say that final causation is a form of efficient causation in which the future acts upon the past, such that the developed form beckons from the future to the past less developed form; rather, the embryonic entity has a structure that develops, if it develops, along a certain line. Thus, final causation and efficient causation, here, are not mutually exclusive, but mutually supportive: the one explaining the emergence of the other, and the other the success and development of the one.[47] What we have here is a development that, barring accidents, will take its course – an evolution that is necessary; its final form immanent as a potentiality within its original one.

The necessity that Marx sees in the line of development of the value-form, is that which Aristotle contrasts with events that are 'accidental', and it is bound up with organic systems and Aristotle's conception of *ousia*. Where there is constant reproduction there is a whole, a system, an *ousia*. Commenting on a passage in Aristotle's *Physics*[48], Stephen Clark writes:

> everything that happens *phusei*, 'by nature', happens always or for the most part, but nothing that happens *apo tuches*, 'by chance', or *apo tautomatou*, 'just of itself', happens thus frequently. Therefore no natural events are thus purely accidental, and therefore all natural events are non-accidental. But all non-accidental events are *heneka tou*, 'serve some purpose', are given sense by their ends. ... Aristotle is not here denying the possibility of something's happening by necessity, as the unpurposed product of natural events ... He is speaking of the persistence of certain types of event or organism ... The fact that rain is always being produced makes

it impossible to doubt that there is an organic system here, and such
systems are 'finalistically' identified. To answer the question 'what
is it?' we must reply in terms of its natural line of development . . .
genesis, the process of coming-to-be, is what it is because *ousia* is
what it is, and not vice versa.[49]

'Coming-to-be (is) therefore a matter of actualizing the
potential of some currently existing entity' or *ousia*.[50]

The proximity of the categories with which Aristotle is
thinking to those with which Marx develops his subject
matter in *Capital* is obvious. For Aristotle, 'we have scientific
knowledge when we know the cause',[51] and 'cause' here
means the form or structure comprehended as the aim or end
(telos, ergon) of a movement or characteristic behaviour,
which is revealed by observation of that movement and
behaviour. Marx's object in *Capital* is to reveal the form and
its necessary line of development; he begins with the simplest
form and presents each subsequent articulation as a development of form. He is able to pursue this method of exposition,
because he had already through the 'method of enquiry'
appropriated the data, the behaviour characteristic of the
organism in its reproduction in the higher form of capitalist
commodity production, and had sought out the Aristotelian
'cause', the form of the underlying development, and the
necessity with which the *ousia* undergoes its metamorphoses
or line of development from its simplest embryonic form.[52]

As Marx puts the term to work in *Capital*, therefore,
'contradiction' is not only something inherent in an essence;
it is, more specifically, a potentiality within the essence which
will, conditions permitting, be realized, and in being realized
will appear in non-accidental or necessary changes that
beget an organic system.

(Perhaps it can be inferred from this, that any area of
reality which enquiry reveals to be a system or organism
with an historical growth, will be susceptible of dialectical
exposition in some form, and will indeed require this for its
more developed scientific presentation. This, perhaps, is the
direction from which to approach the vexed question of the
'dialectic of nature'. Looked at in this way, however, it
becomes an *empirical* matter whether a given sphere of
natural reality is organic in essence or not. If the cogent work

of Bhaskar is right, however, it would seem that such questions are not empirical but that, on the contrary, it is only philosophical error in the bourgeois epoch that generated the idea that natural reality *could* be anything other than an organic system of real essences, or a set of them.[53])

VIII

Dialectics is, then, a method of presentation, but not in the sense of a mere style and arrangement more to the taste of nineteenth-century German sensitivity than 'the gross English manner'. It is a method of presentation whose point lies outside itself, in the nature of the content or subject-matter being presented. For the key to that content is its form and *genesis*, that is, the realization of the potentialities inherent in its embryonic form. The further development of the science consists in showing the necessity of its subsequent transformations into more developed forms, within the ongoing social metabolism *(Stoffwechsel)* in which the daily practice of people develops practical problems and discovers their resolutions. It is the nature, in reality, of the process of *genesis* that imposes requirements and limitations upon the method by which it may adequately be presented.

Thus, referring back to section I above, dialectic is, without paradox, both a movement of the mind, and something mind-independent that imposes itself from the realm of Being. The form and its transformations are *revealed* by enquiry and abstraction, but the form and transformations so revealed *are* (or arise from) the essence of the reality (system or whole) under study. So once the science has been developed 'to the point where one can present it dialectically', one has then to achieve its presentation in that way (dialectically); having traced out the 'inner connexion' in thought, one has then to adequately portray the real process of *genesis* of the forms.

Marx's view of classical political economy was that, though it provided necessary scientific analysis, nonetheless it had a fundamental methodological flaw in its 'analytical method'. It proceeds to analyze 'the form of human life' along 'a course directly opposite to their real development' historically. It does so because it begins, as he puts it in *Capital, post festum* with the results of historical development, the developed forms, already to hand. It proceeds uncritically, therefore, by taking 'the forms which stamp products as commodities' for granted as given natural data for analysis, and 'seeks to give an account, not of their *historical* character . . . but of their content and meaning'.[54] In *Theories of Surplus Value*, Marx explains that the contradictions of classical political economy are 'a necessary consequence of its analytical method, with which criticism and understanding must begin'. Once again the question arises: what further methodological development is needed in order to progress beyond the scientific results of classical political economy? The latter provides the analysis which is 'the necessary prerequisite' for making good its own shortcoming, and that shortcoming lies in the fact that it 'is not interested in elaborating how the various *forms* come into being'. The methodological development that is needed, Marx explains, is a '*genetical* presentation . . . the understanding of *the real, formative process in its different phases*'.[55] If Marx's attempt to lay bare, in the opening sections of *Capital*, the phases of that real formative process (*genesis*, coming-to-be) seems unduly unhistorical and formal, then there is some point in pondering Engels' statement that dialectical method 'is nothing else but the historical method only divested of its historical form and disturbing fortuities'.[56] (It is worth noting, in relation to certain debates that have gone on within Marxism, that the categories being put to work here by Marx in the *Theories of Surplus Value* and, as we saw earlier, in *Capital*, were also centrally employed in the *Economic and Philosophical MSS*. Writing, in the latter work, of the divisions between labour and capital, and between capital and land, and of wages, profits and competition, he says: 'Political economy teaches us nothing about the extent to which these external and apparently accidental circumstances are only the expression of a necessary development. We have seen how exchange itself appears to political economy as an accidental fact.'[57])

It is this capturing of the real formative process in its

essence that constitutes, for Marx, the developed *critical* science. It is the attempt to attain it that makes the method of presentation so crucial a question for him, and which explains the restlessness with which he repeatedly returned to it and the pains that he lavished upon it. Correspondence between Marx and Engels in June 1867 led Marx to add to the first edition of *Capital*, while it was still at the printers, an appendix on 'Die Wertform'[58] for the reader who found dialectical presentation difficult. Further revisions were made to the second German edition, and more still to the French edition when that appeared. Still not content, Marx wanted to revise and 'to formulate many theoretical points more exactly, to insert new ones', and it was only illness and the pressing need to prepare Volume II that caused him to limit the changes to be made in the third edition to those that had already been made in the French one.[59]

Marx's need for a method of presentation that would lay bare the real formative process in its essence may help to explain something else. Today, familiar as one is with the criticisms conventionally made of the labour theory of value, it may be tempting to ask why Marx chose to open *Capital* with what appears to be a problem about a 'common factor' in commodities? Why did he not go straight into social relations of production as he did in the 1859 *Preface*? Had he done so he would have vitiated the now usual criticisms about machines producing value, about reduction of skilled to simple labour and the other usual objections based on incomprehension. Part of the answer must surely begin with the fact that had he done that it would have been very much more difficult for him to portray the process of *genesis* of *forms*, that is the value-forms. It would have been difficult for him to have divested the process of its 'disturbing fortuities', for he would have had to deal with the historical formation of the social relations of market or exchange-based society, through which the product of labour acquires the commodity-form, or value-form. More to the point, he would have had to deal with pre-capitalist social formations, and this was neither his scientific nor political purpose in writing *Capital*. Given his objectives, Marx's conception of history as science required that he begin where he chose;

'What I start out from is the simplest social form in which
the labour product is presented in contemporary society,
and this is the commodity', as he says in the *Notes on Adolph
Wagner*[60]. Properly understood, this leads, as Marx makes it
lead, into the question of the surplus, exploitation and class
in capitalist society. Marx does not go bare-headed at social
relations at the beginning of *Capital*, but it would be ridi-
culous to think that they do not have an important presence.
For his analysis concerns the forms through which exchange
(and with it production) activity and relations develop
(cf. Aristotle's dialectical treatment in *Politics*, I, 9–10).
That again is why he begins with the commodity-form and
not with money as do Ricardo and all bourgeois theory. Indeed, although this is to start a hare which there is no possibility
of pursuing here, Marx's fundamental criticism of Ricardo
is not of his inconsistency or a-historicalness, but of his
failure to grasp the concept of form, that is the value-form.[61]
In *Theories of Surplus Value* Marx acknowledges Ricardo's
understanding of labour as the 'substance, the intrinsic
foundation of their (commodities–S.M.) value ... what
Ricardo does not investigate is the *specific* form in which
labour manifests itself as the common element of
commodities'.[62]

Having traced out the inner connexion, having identified
the embryonic form and comprehended the transformations
through which it moves into higher forms, Marx has then
to reproduce that movement in a communicable manner
without falsifying or misrepresenting it. His expression, and
the organization of the thoughts expressed, had to be such
as would mirror a movement; not just a movement, however,
but one which necessarily follows a certain line. At the
same time, the forms do not exist in reality as static phases
punctuating the movement, and they cannot be represented as if that is what they are. They have no existence apart
from the movement. And yet the essence of the movement lies in the forms and their necessary development, and
comprehending that movement presupposes analysis of
those forms. The exposition of such a reality, both its movements and its forms, presents enormous problems. A movement is best captured by a movie, but an analysis of a form

requires detailed examination of a snapshot. How does one portray a snapshot in movement? Marx was striving to combine the two without detriment to either. This intractable problem of portraying a process of *genesis*, a movement of forms, Marx seems never to have solved to his own satisfaction. The importance he gave to the matter, and his dissatisfaction with his own efforts at grappling with it, have been fully justified by history. Understanding of the nature and full ambition of *Capital*, especially of its opening sections, has been greatly outweighed by non-understanding, and still is.

Notes

1   See Trotsky, *In Defense of Marxism*, 2nd edn. (New York 1973), p. 49.
2   *Dialectical Materialism* (London 1968), pp. 86–109.
3   *Ibid.* p. 111.
4   *Capital*, I. (London 1976), pp. 184–5.
5   G. Kay, 'Why labour is the starting point of *Capital*', *Critique*, VII, pp. 58–9.
6   Trotsky, *loc. cit.*
7   As Martin Nicolaus observes in his Foreword to his translation of *Grundrisse* (London 1973), p. 13.
8   Marx to Engels, dated 16 January 1958 in *Marx, Engels Werke*, (*MEW*), XXIX (Berlin 1967), p. 259; dated 14 January 1858 in *MEGA*, II (Berlin 1930), p. 274.
9   Nicolaus, *ibid.* (see note 7), p. 30.
10 Nicolaus, *ibid.* p. 31.
11 Sean Sayers, 'The Marxist dialectic', *Radical Philosophy*, XIV (Summer 1976), p. 16.
12 Marx to Engels, 1 February 1858 in *MEW*, XXIX, p. 275.
13 *Op. cit.* p. 101.
14 Hegel, *The Science of Logic*, A. V. Millar (trs.) (London 1969), pp. 33, 37ff.
15 Michael Kosok, 'The formalization of Hegel's dialectical logic', in A. MacIntyre (ed.), *Hegel: A Collection of Critical Essays* (London 1976), pp. 237–87.
16 K. Popper, 'What is dialectic?', *Mind* (1940), reprinted in *Conjectures and Refutations*.
17 Roy Edgley, 'Dialectic: the contradiction of Colletti', *Critique*, VII (Winter 1976–7), pp. 49–50.
18 Trotsky, *op. cit.* pp. 49, 50 and 51 respectively.
19 *MEW*, XXX, p. 131.
20 *Ibid.* 578.
21 *Grundrisse*, *loc. cit.*
22 *Ibid.*
23 *Capital*, I, p. 102, 'Postface to the second German edition'.
24 Nothing is revealed or explained by E. Mandel's statements that 'In fact, he starts from elements of the material concrete to go to the theoretical abstract'; Mandel's introduction to the Pelican edition of *Capital*, I, p. 21. His discussion is interesting and suggestive in *Late Capitalism* (London 1975) ch. 1.
25 *Capital*, I, p. 163.
26 *Capital*, I, pp. 153–4.
27 *Ibid.* pp. 139–40, italics added.

28 *Ibid* p. 153.
29 *Loc. cit.*
30 *Ibid.* I, p. 154.
31 *Ibid.* p. 181.
32 *Ibid.* p. 180.
33 *Ibid.* p. 198.
34 *Ibid.* pp. 235–6.
35 L. Colletti, *New Left Review*, 93, (1975).
36 Edgley, *op. cit.* p. 48.
37 Edgley, *op. cit.* p. 47.
38 Aristotle, *Metaphysics*, A II, 982b. 29f.
39 Hegel, *Science of Logic*, p. 35.
40 W. V. O. Quine, *Methods of Logic*, (London 1962) pp. xiii–xiv.
41 Aristotle, *Metaphysics*, VII, 1031bbf.
42 S. Kripke, 'Naming and Necessity', in *Naming, Necessity, and Natural Kinds*, S. P. Schwartz (ed) (New York 1977).
43 Colletti, *op. cit.*, p. 6, quoted from Kant's 'The attempt to introduce the concept of negative quantities into philosophy' of 1763.
44 Quoted by Colletti, *op. cit.*, p. 7.
45 *Capital*, I, p. 198.
46 S. Clark, *Aristotle's Man*, (Oxford 1975), p. 141. In this part of the argument I am much indebted to this original work.
47 *Ibid.* p. 16.
48 Aristotle, *Physics*, II, 198b 33–199a 8.
49 Clark, *op. cit.*, pp. 60–1.
50 *Ibid.* p. 64.
51 *Posterior Analytics*, 71b, 30f.
52 I. Rubin develops a view similar to that adopted here. See his *Essays on Marx's Theory of Value* (Detroit 1972), pp. 42–3 and *passim*.
53 Roy Bhaskar, *A Realist Theory of Science*, originally published by Leeds Books Ltd. (1975), and now re-published by Harvester Press.
54 *Capital*, I, italics added.
55 *Theories of Surplus Value*, III (Moscow 1971), p. 500, italics added.
56 Marx and Engels, *Selected Correspondence*, (London 1941), p. 108.
57 Marx, *Early Writings* (London 1974), p. 323.
58 English translation in *Capital and Class*, IV (Spring 1978).
59 Engels, 'Preface to the Third Edition', *Capital*, I, p. 106.
60 'Notes on Adolph Wagner', in *Karl Marx : Texts on Method*, T. Carver (ed. and trs.) (Oxford 1975), p. 198.
61 I am indebted to Geoffrey Kay for this observation.
62 *Theories of Surplus Value*, III, p. 138.

2 *Marxism and Dialectics**
DAVID-HILLEL RUBEN

> In its rational form [dialectic] ... is a scandal and abomination to
> bourgeoisdom and its doctrinaire professors, because it includes
> in its comprehension and affirmative recognition of the existing
> state of things, at the same time also, the recognition of the negation
> of that state, of its inevitable breaking up; because it regards every
> historically developed social form as in fluid movement, and therefore
> takes into account its transient nature ...

> Marx, 'Afterword to the second German edition',
> *Capital*, Volume I

I

THE relationship between Marx's thought and that of one of
his intellectual parents, Hegel, is not easy to decipher.
Some commentators have thought that Marx added almost
nothing of theoretical interest to what Hegel had already said,
at least not to what Hegel said in his most 'materialist'
moments in *The Phenomenology of Mind* for example.[1]
Others have argued that the mature Marx constituted a
complete 'rupture' or break with Hegelian modes of thought.
There can, I think, be no doubt that neither slogan even
begins to represent the complexity and intricacy of that
relationship. My own view is that, very often anyway, when
Marx bears a resemblance to Hegel terminologically, that
resemblance is *only* superficial; the shared terminology tends
to hide rather than reveal the enormous gulf that separates
them. When Marx uses certain terminology and modes of
expression – and I am thinking here primarily of the vocabulary of the dialectic – sufficiently new content has been

* My thanks to John Mepham for his insightful and helpful criticism of the
ideas expressed in this paper.

built in, or sufficiently old content deleted, to permit us to speak of the important ways in which Marx has moved beyond Hegel's position. Clearly, Marxists – and especially those undertaking an exposition of Marx's methodology – have not always recognized the point that similar terminology can cover dissimilar content. The purpose of this paper is to trace out the way in which one sort of formula, 'concrete identity', changes its meaning from Hegelian to Marxian contexts. In Hegel, the formula presupposes an idealist metaphysic from which it cannot be detached. In Marx, the formula is situated in what I call the method of essential composition and physically necessary function. Indeed, I think that the distinctive terminology of the dialectic, in which I include the ideas of real contradiction, identity-in-difference, polar opposition, and negation of the negation, in Marx's hands, if not Hegel's, can be wholly explicated via those notions. Thus, I think that there is nothing irreducibly important about the terminology of the dialectic in Marx; everything to be said dialectically can be said in other words. It is true that those 'other words' go far beyond the parsimonious vocabulary of the philosophies of classical empiricism, logical positivism, etc. Still, since so many Marxists use dialectical terminology on a par with the magic of 'abracadabra' and related mumbo-jumbo in order to conjure away every really perplexing methodological problem, it is refreshing, in my view, to see that one can, in principle, wholly dispense with the dialectical vocabulary. I will not be able to substantiate my overall point here, but I will try to show how this is to be accomplished for one notion, that of 'concrete identity'. I do not dispute that (what I regard as) the *content* of the dialectic is absolutely crucial for Marx's method; rather, my argument is that the dialectical terminology has no especially sacrosanct status in conveying that content to us.

II

In his philosophy, Hegel contrasts claims of concrete identity with those of abstract identity. Indeed, perhaps no other single point is more important in understanding Hegel's philosophy, since he was fond of distinguishing his philosophy from the philosophy which he called 'the philosophy of abstract identity'. He asserts in his *Logic*:

> Modern philosophy . . . reduces everything to identity. Hence its nickname, the Philosophy of Identity,

and

> Modern philosophy has often been nicknamed the Philosophy of Identity. But as was already remarked it is precisely philosophy, and in particular speculative logic, which lays bare the nothingness of the abstract, undifferentiated identity, known to understanding.[2]

According to Hegel, understanding – which includes ordinary modes of scientific thought – unfolds things as they are in abstract identity, for 'A table of contents is all that understanding gives . . . ',[3] whereas to Reason alone is the truth of identity-in-difference revealed, the identity of each thing with its other.

By abstract identity, Hegel refers to the principle that everything is itself and not another thing, or, as he also expresses it, 'for all A, A = A'.

> The propositions thus arising have been stated as Universal Laws of Thought. Thus, the first of them, the maxim of identity, reads: Everything is identical with itself, A = A; and, negatively, A cannot at the same time be A and not A. This maxim, instead of being a true law of thought, is nothing but the law of abstract understanding . . . Utterances after the fashion of this pretended law (A planet is – a planet; Magnetism is – magnetism; mind is – mind) are, as they deserve to be, reputed silly . . . The logic which seriously propounds such laws and the scholastic world in which they alone are valid have been discredited with practical common sense as well as with the philosophy of reason.[4]

For Hegel, the crux of concrete identity or identity-in-difference is given by the denial of the proposition that A cannot be not-A. But, what does he mean by this? I think that the Hegelian identity-in-difference can only be comprehended when it is recalled that Hegelian philosophy is, thoroughly, a philosophy of the necessary connection between things. It is this necessary connection and dependence that is revealed by reason, by the dialectical mode of comprehension: 'But by Dialectic is meant the in-dwelling tendency outwards by which the one-sidedness and limitation of the predicates of understanding is seen in its true light, and shown to be the negation of them . . . '[5]

The necessary dependence of the latter on the earlier, out of which it develops, for Hegel, applies to all things, whether the 'thing' be ideal, natural, or spiritual. Such dependence of 'later' on 'earlier' is not always a temporal one, and it is not easy to make clear precisely what Hegel does mean in the cases of non-temporal development of, for example, ideas. The quasi-logical 'move' from Being to Nothing is, for Hegel, a move in the ideas themselves, and not just in the movement of our thought from the one to the other. But the point that is important here is merely that Hegelian claims about identity-in-difference are *always* grounded for him in claims about the necessary development of one stage or phase of something into another and the consequent necessary dependence of the latter on the former. I do not say that this exhausts Hegel's meaning, or that this is *all* that Hegel intends by his claims of identity-in-difference. I do not think that one can ever capture all of what Hegel was trying to say by translating his terminology into clearer but non-Hegelian terminology.

That Hegel meant more by identity-in-difference than just necessary development and connection can be seen in the fact that there is no incompatibility whatever between abstract identity and identity-in-difference understood as necessary connection and development, and yet Hegel seemed to think that there was an incompatibility between them. He does not deny that abstract identity had a role to play in thought at the level of ordinary and scientific understanding, finite thought. Its place there was legitimate, so long as it eschewed all metaphysical pretensions. At the level of Reason, though, concrete identity does not so much come to supplement abstract identity but rather to replace it altogether. Each mode of comprehension has its exclusive sphere, but only Reason makes available an ultimately true comprehension of reality. I can make no sense whatever of a claim about a way of thinking which wholly *replaces* abstract identity at any level. But in any event, a philosophy of necessary change and development certainly requires abstract identity as well as concrete identity and so I think we are entitled to infer that Hegel meant more by concrete identity than the rather acceptable content I have thus far attributed to it. As will become apparent, I do not think that Marx means any more by it than this 'acceptable content', and I see no reason whatever for attributing to Marx the ludicrous but Hegelian 'rejection' of abstract identity for any level of thought. The crux of Hegel's critique, then, is in fact against a certain view of the world, a certain metaphysics, which denies real necessity, change, connection, and opposition as features of the world. That is a critique that Marx would share. Hegel unfortunately couples that metaphysics with formal logic and abstract identity, and thereby concludes that he is bound to deny both. I can see no reason to couple formal logic and the metaphysics of contingency, stasis, and atomic individuals and hence no reason to attribute to Marx a rejection of formal logic simply on the ground that he rightly objected to the removal of relationality, necessity, opposition, and development from the world. Hegel was simply mistaken in his assumption that formal logic, and in particular abstract identity, necessarily carries with it all this metaphysical baggage, although it may be that certain philosophical views about formal logic (for example empiricist ones) attempt to join them in this way.

Sometimes, but not always, Hegel conceived of the second, other stage as in some sense an 'opposite' to the first stage. It is not easy to capture what 'opposite' means here, and it certainly does not *always* involve the idea of a contradiction in the sense given to that term by formal logic. However, Hegel does not uniformly put so much emphasis on the oppositeness of the succeeding stage of necessary development to the preceding stage, and this is particularly so in examples drawn from nature rather than society or the realm of ideas:

Apart from this general objectivity of Dialectic, we find traces of its presence in each of the particular provinces and phases of the natural and the spiritual world. Take as an illustration the motion of the heavenly bodies. At this moment the planet stands in this spot, but implicitly it is the possibility of being in another spot; and that possibility of being otherwise the planet brings into existence by moving. Similarly, the 'physical' elements prove to be Dialectical. The process of meterological action is the exhibition of their Dialectic. It is the same dynamic that lies at the root of every other natural process . . .[6]

Thus, in 'A is not-A', sometimes Hegel uses 'not-A' to refer to any state or stage of development which follows the preceding stage according to a natural law – such as a planet being at a different place than it was previously. Often, he uses 'not-A' to refer not only to A's naturally successive phase but to a specially contrasting or appropriately 'opposite' phase of A, as in 'Being is nothingness', 'abstract right . . . is a wrong', 'extreme anarchy and extreme despotism naturally lead to one another',' . . . pain and pleasure pass into each other'.[7] But, again, what connects all these examples of 'A is not-A', statements of identity-in-difference from both the natural and social world, is that all are examples of the necessary development of things ('naturally lead to one another', 'pass into each other'). Many writers have spent so much time in explicating the notion of dialectics, on the contrariness of the phases of development that they have tended to omit all emphasis on what I take to be at least as important an element in the notion – the necessary connection and necessary developments and changes that inhere in all things.

It is clear that, for Hegel, ordinary scientific modes of thought occur at the level of the understanding. As such, science, left to its own devices, could only produce a motionless 'catalogue'. Hegel is quite explicit about this. 'For the facts of science have the aspect of a vast conglomerate, one thing coming side by side with another, as if they were merely given and presented – as in short devoid of all essential and necessary connexion'.[8]

The pigeon-holing process of understanding . . . fails to know (the necessity and notion controlling content) . . . It is not even aware of the need for such insight; if it were, it would drop its schematizing process, or at least would no longer be satisfied to know by way of a mere table of contents . . .[9]

Thus, the nature of the knowledge available in science has always a static quality:

> Thus, in theory, knowledge begins by apprehending existing objects in their specific differences. In the study of nature, for example, we distinguish matters, forces, genera, and the like, and stereotype each in its isolation. Thought is here acting in its analytic capacity, where its canon is identity, a simple reference of each attribute to itself. It is under the guidance of the same identity that the process in knowledge is effected from one scientific truth to another. Thus, for example, in mathematics magnitude is the feature which, to the neglect of any other, determines our advance. Hence, in geometry we compare one figure with another, so as to bring out their identity. Similarly in other fields of knowledge, such as jurisprudence, the advance is primarily regulated by identity. On it we argue from one specific law or precedent to another: and what is this but to proceed on the principle of identity?[10]

Physics, says Hegel, is knowledge of forces, laws and genera 'arranged in orders and classes'.[11] 'It is the weakness of physics that it is too much dominated by the category of identity; for identity is the fundamental category of the understanding.'[12] Science, bound to the method of abstract identity, cannot for Hegel uncover the necessary developments internal to things. By its mode of comprehension, it is forever consigned to providing only a static classification scheme for the systematic arrangement of what it studies.

Why did Hegel think that science was a form of thought which allowed only for abstract identity? I think that this is because, as the quotations above really make quite clear, Hegel thought of science as an enterprise whose basic task it was *to distinguish things one from another* and *to* categorize them. In itself, each science omitted from its ken the necessary connections and dependencies between things and the developmental patterns on which such connections are often founded. That is, for Hegel, the principle of abstract identity is the principle that denies, or at least overlooks, necessary relations:

Now the inadequacy of the thought-determinations used in physics can be traced to [the fact that the content] . . . is split into fragments, into parts which are isolated and detached from each other, devoid of any necessary connection . . . [on the other hand] the determinations of philosophical unity are not indifferent; it is the universality which fulfils itself, and which, in its diamantine identity, also contains difference.[13]

Thus ' . . . it is because the method of physics does not satisfy the notion, that we have to go further'.[14] The particular facts of science must be reviewed by Reason in order 'to be received into philosophy'. 'Physics must therefore work into the hands of philosophy in order that the latter may translate into the notion the abstract universal transmitted by it, by showing how this universal, as an intrinsically necessary whole, proceeds from the Notion.'[15] Philosophy and science have the same facts as objects, but what philosophy can do is to *reveal* the necessary connections and dependencies that hold between things, and the movement on which such connections are established, where before science had only seen a catalogue of items. 'As the Philosophy of Nature is a comprehending treatment, it has as its object the same universal (as does science), but *explicit*, and it considers this universal in its own immanent necessity in accordance with the self-determination of the Notion.'[16] Philosophy and science, or the representatives of Reason and the understanding respectively, constitute different ways of looking at the same thing, the first dialectically and the second undialectically. 'What distinguishes the Philosophy of Nature from physics is more precisely, the kind of Metaphysics used by both of them . . . '[17] The full truth of things lies in the method of philosophy, and must be brought to science from a point external to it. A true comprehension of things, although for Hegel *based* on the empirical sciences, is constituted by looking at things in a way which is itself foreign to those sciences. Nor is science able, by itself, to provide an analysis of the necessary connection of things. The facts of science are not presented as necessarily connected – 'they have the aspect of a vast conglomerate . . . as in short devoid of all essential and necessary connexion', as earlier quoted. When philosophy 'translates into the Notion' the facts of the empirical sciences, it does this, Hegel insists, 'by showing how this universal, or an intrinsically necessary whole, proceeds from the notion'. Neither necessary development nor necessary connection and dependence are available to science; both await the discoveries of a philosophy which renounces abstract identity.

In the passage in *The Philosophy of Nature* from which I have been quoting, Hegel argues that the consequence of understanding nature undialectically is that 'we have straightway established a duality of object and subject and their separation, something here and something yonder. Our intention, however, is rather to grasp, to comprehend nature, to make her ours, so that she is not something alien and yonder'.[18] The identity of subject and object is not, for Hegel, just one concrete identity alongside others revealed by dialectics; rather, it is the central concern, the structuring concrete identity, for his entire philosophy. Hegel's essential philosophical task is to show how subject itself becomes substance or object, ' . . . the emptying of self-consciousness itself establishes thinghood . . . self-consciousness knows this nothingness of the object because on the one hand self-consciousness itself externalizes itself; for in so doing it establishes itself as object . . . sets up the object as itself'.[19] This necessary progression of subject to substance and the realization that substance is only subject in its otherness is the *key* necessary development that informs and motivates the whole of Hegel's philosophy. All development, progression, transformation is part of the overall plan for Spirit to realize itself in its achievement of self-awareness. All things manifest necessary development and connection because they ultimately are manifestations of spirit.

Hegel explicitly asserts that the necessary development that philosophy uncovers in the rigid facts of science is just this necessary development of Idea or Spirit. Thus, speculative thought shows us how 'these contents imitate the action of the original creative thought',[20] and that, after their reception by philosophy, 'these contents are now warranted necessary, and no longer depend on the evidence of facts merely . . . the facts as experienced thus become an illustration and a copy of the original and completely self-supporting activity of thought ... '.[21] Dialectics may make nature and society dance, but not to tunes which they compose. They play the tune, but it is composed elsewhere. We find, in Hegel, a profound appreciation of the dynamic necessary tendencies that inform things and their complicated tissue of interrelations, but this appreciation is coupled with an idealist thesis which locates the source of that change and connection not in things inherently, but only in things insofar as they are expressions of the externalizing activity of Spirit. In short, it is the identity of subject and object which grounds all necessary movement and hence which grounds all other claims of concrete identity. The history of the movements of Idea or Subject through all its stages supports, in Hegel's mind, all the other identities-in-difference that there are. 'True scientific knowledge [now philosophy] ... demands abandonment to the very life of the object, or ... claims to have before it the inner necessity controlling the object, and to express this only.'[22] However, the life and vitality of those things come in the final analysis from a source which is not strictly speaking outside them only because they are, in turn, as the 'other' of that source, only manifestations of the very source itself in its otherness. They move because they are concretely identical with the source of Motion itself, Spirit. As Hegel himself puts this point in *The Philosophy of Nature*:

> Nature is to be regarded as a *system of stages*, one arising necessarily from the other and being the proximate truth of the stage from which it results: but it is not generated *naturally* out of the other but only in the inner Idea which constitutes the ground of Nature. Metamorphosis pertains only to the notion as such, since only its alteration is development.[23]

Lukacs saw clearly that, for Hegel, the necessary movement of nature and society constituted merely a pseudo-history of movement, whose authentic history was to be located elsewhere: for Hegel, 'nature is an eternal externalization, its movement is a pseudo-movement, a movement of the subject: in Hegel's theory, nature has no real history'.[24] Similarly, says Lukacs, for history itself in Hegel's philosophy: 'This amounts to the self-annulment of history ... its immanent reality is also annulled: history does not contain its own real, autonomous laws of motion ... '[25] This is because, as Lukacs correctly observes, all oppositions which could otherwise account for movement are themselves rooted and ultimately resolved for Hegel in the single over-arching contradiction of subject and object, and are only manifestations or appearances of that one resolved opposition. 'The spirit which is supposed to make history and whose very essence is supposed to be the fact that it is the actual driving force, the motor of history, ends up by turning history into a mere simulacrum.'[26] History and nature move for Hegel, but only because they are the motions of another, the expressions of oppositions that are not ultimately their own.

III

In Marx, too, one finds claims, occasionally, of concrete identity and, more often, of necessary connection, necessary development, organic interaction, and related expressions. In his well-known discussion of certain methodological questions in the 'Introduction to the *Grundrisse*' he asserts: 'Production is simultaneously consumption as well'; 'The identity of production and consumption amounts to Spinoza's proposition: *Determinatio est negatio*'; 'Production is thus at the same time consumption, and consumption is at the same time production. Each is simultaneously its object'; 'Production is consumption and consumption is production'; ' ... each of them is not only simultaneously the other ... but each of them by being carried through creates itself as the other ... '; and finally: 'After this, nothing is easier than for a Hegelian to answer that production and consumption are identical'; 'The identity of consumption and production has three aspects'.[27] That at least some things are necessarily connected or related seems borne out by the following remark in *Wage-Labour and Capital* : 'Thus capital presupposes wage labour; wage labour presupposes capital. They reciprocally condition the existence of each other; they reciprocally bring forth each other,' or, ' ... capital and wage labour are two sides of the same relation. The one conditions the other, just as userer and squanderer condition each other'.[28] Finally, that in some sense Marx thought that the development of capitalism displayed necessity has shocked many schooled on a diet of Hume on causality; Marx speaks of the development of capitalism as displaying 'the inexorability of a law of nature',[29] and this necessitarian talk is something he uses repeatedly in his descriptions of capitalist development.

It is quite obvious, even on casual inspection, that Marx is here tacitly employing methodological assumptions that are not those of empiricism, positivism, or related modes of thought. Others have too readily used the evidence of this non-empiricist terminology to place him within the tradition of Hegelian philosophy. Superficially at least, they seem similar to the Hegelian claims we have just been discussing. We know, of course, that Marx in *Capital*, Volume I, deliberately toyed with Hegelian modes of expression: 'I therefore openly avowed myself the pupil of that mighty thinker, and even here and there, in the chapter on the theory of value, coquetted with the modes of expression peculiar to him.'[30] Do these claims of necessary connection and development, and concrete identity place the mature Marx within the parameters of Hegelian philosophy? And what in any case is 'necessary connection' or 'necessary dependence'? Are these, as Bertell Ollman has argued,[31] quasi-logical notions which place both Hegel and Marx in the tradition of what Ollman has called 'the philosophy of internal relations'? Or, alternatively, can we understand Marx's method in a way which does not reduce it either to a variety of Hegelianism or to any form of empiricism as this has classically been understood, but rather allows us to appreciate it as a genuine alternative to both those modes of thinking?

My argument here will fall roughly into two parts. First, I want to try to show how talk of concrete identity can be rephrased without remainder into talk of necessary dependence and composition. Now, Marx himself was very much less given to such claims than was Hegel, although they are not wholly absent from his writings either. My real target here, though, is not Marx, but those Marxists who—following

Lukacs I suppose – seem to feel some urge to talk of the identity of subject and object. It is primarily to that issue that I will address myself. Second, having eliminated concrete identity in favour of what I call the method of necessary dependence (or development) and structure, I want to do what I can to explain and make plausible what I take to be Marx's views on those topics. Although I think that all the notions of the dialectic can be similarly eliminated in favour of talk of necessary dependence, development, and (I would add) opposition, I can only hope to make out the case here for the idea of concrete identity. But I do think that the whole of the content that Marx builds into his dialectical vocabulary can be expressed in these other terms.

To turn to our first task, consider those remarks on concrete identity from 'The Introduction to the *Grundrisse*', which have been quoted. Marx's discussion in these passages is very complicated, but, as he clearly asserts, he means precisely three distinct things by 'the identity' of production and consumption ('has three aspects').

In the first sense, Marx says that production and consumption are immediately identical. In producing something, a man also consumes something else (for example his own abilities, raw materials), and in consuming things, he also produces something else (for example his own body). In this sense, Marx also says that not all consumption is productive consumption, and not all production is consumptive production. Hence, this immediate unity 'lets their immediate duality persist' and in general he seems to dismiss this point.

In the second sense of their identity, a 'non-immediate' sense, a 'mediating movement' takes place between the two. 'Production mediates consumption . . . Consumption also mediates production . . . Without production, there is no consumption; however, without consumption there is no production.' In this sense, Marx says that consumption and production supply the object for one another. Production creates the material objects of consumption; consumption creates the 'ideal' or 'conceptual' object of production by creating 'the need for new production, a reason which is a presupposition of production . . . it creates the object which is active in production of a purpose-defining object'. Above it was shown that, in the first sense of the identity of production and consumption, Marx says that their duality persists. In this sense, too, although they are related to one another and indispensible for one another, 'they still remain external'.

Finally, in the third sense, 'each of the two creates the other as it is carried out'. Marx meant several things by this third sense of identity of production and consumption. First, a necessary condition for something's being a 'real' product is that it is consumed, 'since only in consumption does the product become a real product'. Second, through consumption a need for new production is brought about and hence certain productive skills are 'produced'. Third, the precise way in which things are produced determines the methods or forms that consumption takes, and the specific desires to consume what has in fact been produced. If the second sense of identity can be characterized as that each provides the *material* for the other, the third is concerned with the ways in which each provides the *form* for the other. The form that production takes in a society (viz. new productive skills) is in part determined by consumption, and production determines in part the forms that consumption takes (viz. new desires for and new forms of consumption). Marx says that this third sense of identity 'is illustrated many times in (political) economy in the relation of supply and demand, of objects and needs, of needs created by society and natural needs'.

After concluding his discussion of these three senses of the identity of production and consumption, Marx makes this anti-Hegelian remark:

> After this nothing is easier for a Hegelian than to posit production and consumption [as] identical ... The important [point, though] to be emphasized here is that ... they appear in any case, as moments of a process in which production is the real starting point and of which it is also the transcending moment.

Now, nothing in any of this, as far as I can see, escapes expression in the relatively humdrum language of necessary dependence, connection, or development. Certainly, Marx

himself says that the first two senses of 'identity' leave
production and consumption in their duality external to one
another. What then is the upshot of the third sense? Marx
shows the ways in which the character of production and
consumption are necessarily dependent, the one on the other,
or the ways in which they presuppose the other ('for only
in consumption does the product become a real product'),
or ways in which one of the pair necessarily develops into
the other (consumption is 'the act through which the producer
becomes a product'). Thus, at least here, we can capture *all*
of what Marx intends by his claims of concrete identity
without employing that peculiar 'dialectical' notion at all,
by using instead only his notion of necessary connection,
dependence, or development. That we can do this genuinely
distinguishes Marx's dialectic from Hegel's in at least one
important respect. At least for 'concrete identity', Marx has
succeeded in detaching it from the Hegelian metaphysic of
Absolute Spirit, and posed for us the possibility of rendering
it lucid 'in other words'. What Marx offers us is a *science* of
the necessary phases and stages of production, not one awaiting philosophy in order to import necessity and development
from the outside. I think it can be conjectured that Marx
himself was aware of the discrepancy between the Hegelian
jargon of the text and the content he built into the jargon,
and that it was this awareness that led him to say that,
whereas a Hegelian might posit the identity of production
and consumption, what was alone important was to see how
they were linked as 'moments of a process'.

Before turning to some constructive remarks on these
'other words' which so crucially involve the recurring
adjective 'necessary', I want to make some further points
about that very special concrete identity of subject and
object. Special for whom? Nor for Marx, for he never uses
such an expression. He does say the following: 'Thus society
is the consummated oneness in substance of man and nature';
'It will be seen how subjectivism and objectivism, spiritualism
and materialism, activity and suffering, only lose their
antithetical character ... in the social condition.'[32] But
these remarks simply make the point that society is the
meeting place of man and nature – social products are

nature 'touched' by human subjectivity. They have nothing to do with concrete identity.

We saw how central the identity of subject and object was to Hegel's philosophy. Ultimately, for Hegel, the necessary development of subjectivity to objectivity and the necessary dependence of the latter on the former is explicated by the creative role played by Absolute Spirit in bringing forth a natural world. Such talk of the identity of subject and object has certainly found a second home within certain currents of Marxism, as well as other modes of philosophizing. Does such an identity have a legitimate place within a materialist philosophy, or does it retain irreducibly idealist implications?

Lukacs, to my mind the most sensitive and able Marxist philosopher that Marxism has yet produced, waivered in his answer to that question. In his early 'Reification and the Consciousness of the Proletariat', the proletariat can become the identical subject–object of history, the practical resolution of one of the central antinomies of bourgeois thought. Both in a footnote to 'What is Orthodox Marxism?' and in the concluding pages of the Reification essay, Lukacs limits the identity claim to social existence, to history:[33] 'the proletariat is the identical subject–object of the history of society';[34] in nature, 'dialectics ... can never become more exalted than a dialectics of movement witnessed by the detached observer ... '[35] On the other hand, in his much later *The Young Hegel*, Lukacs says without qualification that ' ... the identical subject–object is the central pillar of objective idealism ... ',[36] and claims that Schelling's and Hegel's 'search for an objective-idealist dialectic forces them to take the mystification of an identical subject–object really seriously'.[37] The identity of subject and object has ceased to be the truth of history: ' ... the attempt to abolish reality's character as real, to transmute objectivity into something posited by the subject and into an identity of subject and object, in short to complete the transformation of substance into subject',[38] this now, according to Lukacs, can be the only result of the identity of subject and object.

Who was correct, the early or late Lukacs? Lukacs himself, as far as I know, never clearly states what is involved in an identity claim about subject and object, so that it is never certain what is implied by his acceptance or rejection of it. It is this that I want to pursue briefly now.

I have tried to explain such claims of concrete identity in Marx by way of the notions of necessary development and dependence. For Hegel, there was such a necessity that inhered in Absolute Spirit, for its necessary development included the history of its objectification in a natural world, and its self-conscious reclamation of that world as its own. For a materialist, there could be no history of necessary development from subjectivity to objectivity. No individual subject, nor even an absolute one, has a history which includes its objectification in a natural world. Such a conception is wholly idealist.

Now, one of the major thrusts of Marx's science of society is to de-naturalize that which needed to be de-naturalized, in the sense of 'natural' which makes it that which is essentially independent of man. Marx correctly pinpointed a pervasive, deep tendency within especially (but not only) bourgeois thought to de-humanize certain features of our experience and to treat them *as if* they were natural. The task of science was to 'unlock the secret' that such things are also human phenomena. First and foremost, he considers value.

> The recent scientific discovery, that the products of labour, so far as they are values, are but material expressions of the human labour spent in their production, marks, indeed, an epoch in the history of the development of the human race, but by no means dissipates the mist through which the social character of labour appears to us to be an objective character of the products themselves.[39]

That the value of commodities, apparently natural, is essentially the expression of human labour power, Marx treats as his most important scientific finding. Value belongs on the human side of things, not on the natural, and the import of Marx's discovery was to relocate value from its mislocation by bourgeois political economy.

But we render to Caesar that which is Caesar's and to God that which is God's. On the one hand, I have described Marx's efforts to re-anthropomorphize things like value, which are essentially human, and which had been wrongly naturalized. Equally, though, the thrust of Marx's philosophy, on the other hand, is to refuse to allow the *whole* of the objective, natural world to be swallowed up by subjectivity, and this he accomplishes by disallowing the anthropomorphization of everything. If the former effort is in reply to bourgeois political economy, the latter effort is by way of reply to Hegel.[40] Marx then attempts to steer between the Scylla of naturalizing the human and the Charybdis of subjectifying the legitimately natural. A balance must be struck in an exposition of Marxism – a balance between the unacceptable extremes of claiming everything for subjectivity as did Hegel, and the other, bourgeois extreme of treating the human as only a natural, often eternal, feature of the objective order. The fault of Hegel's 'subject is object' is that it errs on the idealist side, for according to it all objects are mere developments and hence expressions of subjectivity. Whatever his intentions may have been, the formulations of the early Lukacs on the identity of subject and object carry with them the themes of these Hegelian errors. It is true that sometimes the early Lukacs seems only to mean, when he speaks of the proletariat as being the identical subject – object of history, that only the proletariat as a class is capable of achieving self-knowledge about its true role in history. But if this is all that it means, why not say it in these words? Talk of subject – object identity tends to confuse rather than enlighten. We prefer the understanding of the latter Lukacs on this point of terminology.

Briefly, I want to distinguish this point from a somewhat similar point made recently by Lucio Colletti, in his *Marxism and Hegel*.[41] Colletti locates the source of Hegel's idealism, his annihilation of matter, in his assertion that finite, material reality, has its essence in its other, the immaterial infinite. Thus, to speak in the language of concrete identity, the finite is the infinite, matter is ideal. As Colletti sums up Hegel's point: 'The finite "is not" when it is really finite; vice versa, it "is" when it "is not", it is "itself" when it is the "other", it comes to birth when it dies. The finite is dialectical.'[42] 'The finite has as its essence and foundation what is "other" than itself.'[43] Now, Colletti rightly observes that the consequence of *this* concrete identity is that the material world has, for Hegel, disappeared. What Colletti infers from this is that the dialectical view of matter is inherently idealist. This is an error. I have tried to discover something in Hegel's texts, the notions of necessary development and change, which could be used by a materialist philosophical outlook. These notions do not exhaust Hegel's meaning of dialectics which, for him, is connected with an idealist metaphysic. But there is no reason why that which is rational in Hegel's dialectic cannot be used by materialism, and further, that which is rational can be explicated by the notions of necessary connection, development, and opposition where those notions themselves retain their distinctive integrity and are not given some Humean or empiricist reductive analysis. The terminology of the dialectic is not important, but its rational content is. It is this which Colletti tends to underplay in his critique of the Hegelian dialectics of matter. What Colletti asserts is that Engels, Plekhanov, and Lenin carry over in their dialectical materialism the implicit idealism of Hegel. But really Colletti presents no textual evidence for this. He quotes Engels' assertion that we must consider 'things in their motion, their change, their life, their reciprocal influence on one another', and in general the passages he cites from these materialists are those that stress the change and dynamic tendencies inherent in all things, all of which is perfectly acceptable to a materialist. There is no special reason why a materialist outlook should not stress the necessary development, opposition, and change in things – which is what Engels as well as Marx took to be the rational core of the dialectic – without also asserting that the finite necessarily develops or changes into the infinite, or subject into object; only the latter of which are genuinely idealist formulations. There is no reason to reject all claims of identity-in-difference, properly understood, on the grounds that specific ones, like the identity of subject and object or of finitude and infinity, are idealist.

IV

The second task which I earlier set myself was to explain,

defend, and make plausible at least some of the notions that have been used in the description of Marx's method. I cannot hope to deal with all of the concepts that would have to be used in explaining the terminology of the Marxian dialectic in other words. For example, setting out the dialectic in other words will need the conception of a necessary opposition. This is one of the many conceptions about which I have, here, nothing to say.

What has been repeated in all the phrases used in the exposition of Marx's method is the word 'necessary'. What sort of necessity is this? Is it logical necessity, such that if two things necessarily depend on one another then there is no possible world in which one could exist without the other?[44] Or is the necessity physical or natural?

It is obvious that the necessities so far discussed – necessary dependence, development, change, and connection – are physical necessities, for it is not logically impossible that things might not have depended on, lead from, or been connected to, whatever in fact it is on which they are so dependent, resultant, or connected. It is not logically impossible that production might not provide the form consumption takes. Indeed, in terms of logical impossibility, it is not even impossible that the material object of consumption did not arise from production – for there might have been a manna of all consumer items miraculously sent from heaven into the hands of the appropriate consumer. What needs to be argued for in order to set out in any authentic way the methodology of Marx is a notion of physically necessary dependence, change, connection or relation, which is weaker than the notion of logical necessity but stronger than the standard empiricist regularity reconstructions of those ideas. I am not asserting that the 'source' of the necessity is different in the two cases, for example that one is *de dicto* or conventional, the other *de re* or real. All that is claimed is that some sort of distinction is needed here, and that there is a *difference*, however it is to be characterized, for example between the necessities of capitalist development on the one hand and the necessities of self-identity on the other.[45]

The old notion of an internal relation is used ambiguously

to cover two different sorts of necessity, the logical and the physical. Ollman, for instance, who places Marx so squarely in the tradition of internal relations, never says clearly which sort of necessity is involved in an internal relation. Insofar as an internal relation is taken as a logically necessary one, it can be rejected as an account of what Marx means here, although I shall be returning to a discussion of whether the notion of logical necessity might have some other auhentic place within the ambit of Marx's ideas. On the other hand, if an internal relation is taken as one of physical necessity, what follows can be read as a development of that idea.

For Marx, the questions of whether necessity was part of our understanding of notions like causal dependence or whether it was to be replaced with some regularity surrogate, and whether such necessity was something *real* in the world or whether it was merely something contributed by the human mind, were not for him in fact live questions. For the philosophical milieu in Germany that immediately followed Kant, the question of the irreducibility of a notion of physical necessity to any Human replacement had been settled by Kant. Further, the belief that such physical necessity was real rather than mental is already a theme in Feuerbach's critique of Kant which Marx knew and, I think, accepted.[46] How far necessity encroached on human freedom was still problematic, but I think Marx would have taken for granted that however far science, whether natural or human science, could extend itself, that far was the realm of physical necessity to be accorded a place. For Marx, as for the entire milieu in which he writes, to say that two things are dependent or interconnected or that one develops from the other *is* to speak of physically necessary interconnection, development or dependence. That necessity is a physical necessity in things, or *de re* physical necessity as it is now called. Things are governed by necessity, and laws summarize this. Our talk of necessity in necessary development derives its content from this real, natural necessity in things which is responsible for how they develop and behave. Such a conception of the scientific investigation of physical necessities has as much place for Marx in the social as the natural order, although some of the initial hostility that might be felt to this should dissipate when I discuss the *tendential* nature of such necessities for Marx.

For philosophers schooled in the tradition of Hume, such physical necessitarian talk amounts either to obfuscation or outright anthropomorphism. There is no doubt whatever that it is an integral part of how Marx understood what he was doing. But two questions can be asked about such talk of physical necessity. First, why is it thought that it is necessary to talk in such a way? What does such physical necessitarian talk accomplish that more prosaic regularity talk does not accomplish? Second, even if it is thought that talk of physical necessity is useful, how is such talk to be explicated or analyzed?

First, what does talk of physical necessity do that talk of constant conjunction of events does not do? The intuitive idea here is that necessities restrict possible alternatives open to us,[47] and that this idea is not one that can be fully comprehended on a regularity analysis of causal dependence or development. Marx quotes, in the 'Introduction to the *Grundrisse*', Spinoza's dictum that *determinatio est negatio*. When something is determined to be something, or to act in some way, certain alternatives are closed off to that thing. Just as acorns are determined to become oaks and not beech trees, so also late capitalism is determined to develop a monopoly stage and not petty commodity production. What physical necessity offers is a way of seeing the world with restricted possibilities and options, and sets the task of tailoring action to fit in with the physical necessities that do make some things impossible.

When Engels said that freedom is the insight into necessity, it was just this intuition that he was trying to capture. For Marx and Engels, scientific socialism was distinguished from utopian socialism in just this way – the vision of the future was founded on the real (physical) possibilities inherent in the present. Physical possibilities, impossibilities, and necessities, both natural and social, set the parameters for rational action. No account of development, change, or transition which does not include a conception of real, physical necessity or possibility could possibly be adequate for understanding what the world is like, what science is like, or what rational activity or praxis is.

This argument assumes not only that one speaks in terms of physical necessity, possibility, and impossibility, but also – as I said – 'that this idea is not one that can be fully comprehended on a regularity analysis of causal dependence or development'. That is, it is assumed that there is no successful reductionist account of 'physically could' in terms of something else which itself does not assume the idea of physical possibility in its own analysis. At first, M.R. Ayers seems to be offering just such a reductionist account.[48] Ayers proposes that 'X can do A' means 'In some circumstances, X would do A' (p. 69), and later this is amended to 'under some circumstances, X will do A' (p. 80). Thus, if causal possibility were analysable into conditionals of this straightforward form, it would seem to present no special difficulty of comprehension to the regularity analyst.

Now, it is obvious, as it stands, that such an analysis will not work. The antecedent clause of the analysans is ambiguous between 'under some logically possible circumstances' and 'under some causally possible circumstances'. The antecedent cannot be taken in the first way, since that would render almost everything within A's power, since A could do (almost) anything under *some* logically possible set of circumstances. But if the antecedent is taken in the latter way, the explication or analysis is patently circular. Ayers himself considers just this objection, and concludes 'that we have not succeeded in explaining potentiality away in terms of something else' (p. 88). Ayers seems undisturbed at the outcome, on the grounds that to explain a concept does not entail reduction but location of that concept within a family of interrelated concepts, and that 'we need not expect that all the species are reducible to one of their own number without differentiae. It is nevertheless important to find ways of demonstrating the more or less subtle relationships that exist within the genus' (p. 88). Having travelled this far with Ayers, in the expectation that something more than this was to be proferred, it may come as a surprise that this is all that is on offer. Of course, there is nothing wrong with the idea that the best one can do in many instances of concept explication is to place the concept within its interrelated family. Ultimately, such a procedure has a circularity about it, but this may be acceptable. But for genuine illumination to occur, it can be demanded that the circle be wider than 'it is physically possible that X do A' iff 'under some physically possible circumstances, X will do A'. That seems to be not so much concept explanation (even within a circular family) as concept repetition.

Second, how shall sense be made out of talk of physical necessity? Can we give it an analysis or explication? Part of the problem in answering this question is to understand such a request, or what should count as reasonable criteria for having made sense of something. If a so-called 'reductive' explication is being sought, an analysis which explains the notion of physically necessary dependence, connexion, etc., *without* using other notions in the analysans which, in turn, rely for their analysis on the notion of physical necessity, then such an account may well be impossible. It ought not to be a surprise, if it was the case as Ayers suggested, that many terms participate in a circular family of such terms, such that the explication of any one relies, in some sense, on at least one of the other family members. This has certainly been claimed for 'analyticity' and 'logical possibility'. Hence, it might be that no member of such a family can be given a reductive analysis which uses no related members, and this may apply to 'physically necessary' too.

There have been at least two attempts in recent philosophical literature to clarify physical necessity, and I want to comment briefly on these.[49] Both attempt to define physical necessity as what holds in some proper subset of the logically possible worlds. Thus, physical necessity is weaker than logical necessity on such an account, yet takes us beyond the merely actual.

First, we can try to explain physical necessity by applying David Lewis's discussion of the truth conditions for counterfactual assertions. Now, it is logically necessary that if p, then q if and only if in every possible world in which p is true, q is true. Such an explication is not reductive, since clearly any explication of possible world talk will, ultimately, require the reintroduction of the notion of what is logically necessary. In a parallel fashion, it can be said that it is physically necessary that if p, then q, if and only if in all possible worlds most like the actual world in which p is true, q is true, and 'if p, then q' is not true in all possible worlds.

Second, there has been an attempt by Karl Popper to explain physical necessity: 'a statement is physically necessary if and only if . . . [it is true] in all worlds that differ from our world, if at all, only with respect to initial conditions.'[50] The idea is that what is physically necessary is what stays true in those worlds which are just like ours except that the initial conditions may vary from those which obtain(ed) in our world.

Now, it is clear that in both attempts there exists a *sort* of circularity. J.L. Mackie for example, says, that Popper's account does not seem 'very illuminating. Since "initial conditions" are simply what we contrast with laws of working (laws of natural necessity), this means that what is physically necessary holds in all worlds that have the same laws of working as our own . . . '[51] Similar accusations of circularity have been brought against Lewis's explication in terms of relative similarity between possible worlds, since judgments of comparative similarity rest on previous intuitions about the relative weighing that is to be given to the importance of nomic and non-nomic differences between possible worlds. If there is a nomic relationship between p and q, then q is true in all those possible worlds most like the actual world in which p is true. This entails that there is *no* possible world in which p is true but q is false which is more like the actual world than that world which is most like the actual world in which p and q are both true. Now consider that world most like the actual world in which p and q are true. In the strictly counterfactual case in which p and q are actually false, that world we are now considering is unlike the actual world insofar as in it (but not in the actual world) p and q are true (and of course, that world is also unlike the actual world in any respect which is entailed by p or q). Further, consider a possible world in which p is true but q is false which is as much like the actual world as possible. That world will differ from the actual world in only *one* respect, namely, the truth of p (and of course will differ in any respect entailed by p), for in that world q will be false, just as it is in the actual world. But what must be said, if the explication is correct, is that any world which differs from the actual world in only one respect of particular fact, viz. the truth of p, is less like the actual world than a world unlike the actual world in two respects of particular fact, the truth of p and q. The intuition that this is so, which will make the two sides of the analysis truth-functionally equivalent, must rest on the belief that in the latter, but not in the former, a nomic connection is preserved. That is, nomic facts outweigh particular ones in importance in assessing relative similarities between possible worlds.

Thus, nomic differences must be treated as more weighty in establishing similarity and dissimilarity across possible worlds than non-nomic ones. However, this does not show that the *explication* of 'physically necessary that' is circular, since the argument I have just sketched does not establish that nomicality would re-arise in the explication of 'more similar' or 'more importantly similar' as applied to possible worlds. The explication assumes that these we will *in fact* find nomic differences more important than non-nomic ones, and if this is something about which there is general agreement, this itself vitiates Mackie's other charge that Lewis has failed to supply determinate truth-conditions for such analyses, apparently on the grounds that people *will* disagree in assessments of relative importance of similarities and dissimilarities.[52] In any event, that it is assumed that there will be general agreement about such assessments of overall similarity and that nomic differences will count as weightier does not by itself make the explication of physical necessity by overall similarity circular in the traditional sense of that accusation.

Similar remarks can be made in defence of Popper against Mackie. 'Initial conditions' can be explained or identified without reference to laws of natural necessity. It may be that initial conditions are in fact 'what we contrast with laws of working', but it does not follow that the idea of explicating 'physical necessity' by means of initial conditions involves a circularity in the traditional sense.

Even *if* such attempts were involved in straight definitional circularity, this would not necessarily vitiate such explications, assuming that the circles were large enough. Many have argued, as I quoted Ayers, that this is just what we should expect from concepts that exist only as a member of an interdefined family and for which reductive analyses are not possible. My criticism of Ayers was not that such circularity was unacceptable but only that his circle was ludicrously restricted. I would submit, though, that the philosophical difficulties of these issues have less to do with any problem lurking in the concept of physical necessity and much more to do with how to understand what it is to understand or explicate any concept or idea whatever.

In the explications of both Lewis and Popper, physical or natural necessity, although stronger than actual regularity, differs in sense from the still stronger notion of logical necessity. This has been denied by Milton Fisk, who argues that 'I see, then, no reason to distinguish logical from physical necessity as regards necessity'.[53] His argument against Popper's distinction between two kinds of necessity runs as follows: Popper infers that they are different from the premiss 'that though logical necessities hold in all possible worlds physical necessities fail in some possible worlds'. This is precisely the difference I have attributed to them thus far. Fisk argues that the premiss is false, on the grounds that, 'typically physical necessities involve three things, two properties and a kind. The two properties are necessarily connected as properties of things of that kind, but not perhaps as properties of things of a different kind . . . '

Suppose we assert that, of things of natural kind N, necessarily if they have property F, they have property G. Is this true in *all* possible worlds? Fisk reminds us that to say that it is true in *all* possible worlds is not to deny that there is a possible world in which F and G are not necessarily connected, because in that world kind N might be replaced by, or supplemented with, things of some other kind N', in which F and G are not necessarily connected. But, he reminds us, it does not follow from any of this that, as applied to things of kind N, the connection between F and G fails in some possible world. Hence, he asserts that, of things of natural kind N, necessarily (in all possible worlds) if they have F, they have G.

Now, even making this distinction between the two claims does not imply that physical necessities are true in all possible worlds. The result follows only if F and G are properties which are *essential* for things of that kind. That is, assume that there is some distinction to be drawn between properties which things of a kind have essentially, and properties which things have non-essentially. Thus, if F, or G, or being G if F, is a property which a thing of kind N has essentially, then if a thing is of that kind, then it is F, or G, or G if F, in all possible worlds. But the same result certainly does not follow if these properties are had only non-essentially by things of kind N. Not all physical laws are about the *essential* properties had by things of natural kinds, and when they are not, they are not true, even as applied only to things of that natural kind, in all possible worlds.

This distinction vitiates Fisk's argument to what I regard in any case as a true conclusion, viz. that being of a natural kind is not a contingent matter. Fisk argues by *reductio* on the repeated supposition that 'there were a world in which this object that is in actuality a grain of salt were a diamond'. He then infers that if it is a grain of salt in this world, then necessarily (in all possible worlds) it dissolves in water, and hence it dissolves in water in the world in which it is a diamond. But since diamonds necessarily do not dissolve in water, 'we reach a contradiction', and hence if a thing is of a natural kind, then it is of that kind in all possible worlds. But, again, the argument founders on the supposition that a grain of salt which dissolves as a matter of physical necessity in this world does so in all possible worlds. This would be so, I submit, only if the physically necessary property of salt, viz. solubility in water, were had by it essentially, and for this stronger requirement Fisk offers no argument whatever.

I conclude, then, that the attempt to distinguish between physical and logical necessity as two kinds of necessity has not been shown by Fisk to be an ill-founded distinction, although by so distinguishing them I do not suppose either that one is real and the other 'psychological', or 'conceptual', or 'linguistic'. Both are real, but also really different. Indeed, from what I have said, or intimated, they are both real – logical necessities being based on essential, physical necessities on non-essential, properties. That these two necessities are different in the range of possible worlds in which they hold certainly 'fits' our intuitions, for it seems absurd to suggest, as would Fisk, that none of the scientific laws we in fact have – about *our* natural kinds – could have been different than they are, even when they remain about *those* natural kinds.

It is worth noting another account on which all nomic properties of natural kinds, other than those which are concerned with the sorts of sensations that those natural kinds induce in percipients, turn out to be true of things of those natural kinds in all possible worlds.[54] Colin McGinn has argued that,

> properties of a kind come in two grades, one more fundamental than the other. Let's call properties of the more fundamental grade *primary* nomic properties, and let's call properties of the less fundamental grade *secondary* nomic properties ... We know what the nature of a substance is when we have identified its primary properties and seen how they account for the more readily discernible secondary properties.

McGinn then argues that such 'accounting' proceeds by repeated reductive identification of the secondary properties with the primary properties, and, since true identities are necessary and 'property identities, though discovered *a posteriori*, are necessary', these secondary properties are as much part of the essence of a natural kind as are the primary properties with which they are identified. If the primary properties are true of a natural kind in all possible worlds, then so are the secondary properties. 'Whence it follows that if gold couldn't have lacked its atomic properties, it couldn't have lacked its dispositional properties either. For to lack one would just *be* to lack the other.'

McGinn's argument in fact shows that *if* a natural kind has a primary property in all possible worlds, and if that primary property is identical with a secondary property, then the natural kind has the secondary property in all possible worlds. McGinn never establishes the first assumption, and when considered it turns out not to be a very plausible assumption. He characterizes the primary properties of a thing as those which 'underlie' or 'are responsible for' the secondary properties, or those from which the secondary properties are derivative. He then moves on to say, without argument, that the internal nature of a thing 'is constituted by its primary properties'. That is, McGinn simply assumes that all the primary nomic properties of a substance or kind are had by it essentially, in all possible worlds. But this is not very plausible, for there seems nothing at all objectionable about the idea that primary nomic properties themselves come in two kinds, the essential and the non-essential. Whether a secondary nomic property is had by things of a kind essentially or non-essentially, in all possible worlds or in less than all, depends on which sort of primary nomic property it is identified with. There is no *a priori* reason to believe that the nomic properties of a kind which are 'primary', in the sense that they are the smallest set of properties which can be used to account for all the remaining properties (which is the way in which McGinn introduces the idea), are, *all* of them, had by that kind in all possible worlds. Having a certain atomic number may be an essential property of a substance, that is had by that substance in every possible world. It does not follow that every 'internal' or 'atomic' property of a kind – for example, that it emits a certain radiation or that a certain electron jump occurs under given conditions – must be had by that kind also in every possible world. I conclude, then, that neither McGinn nor Fisk has offered any reason for thinking that nomic properties (even aside from those related to the occurrence of appropriate sensations in percipients) are had by a kind in all possible worlds, and that there is no reason to agree with Fisk's refusal to distinguish *logical* from *natural* necessity.

V

There are four related points about Marx's conception of physical necessity at least as it is applied to understanding society that I wish to discuss. These are: (1) physical necessity relates to individuals; (2) such necessity is tendential; (3) tendencies arise from the 'nature' of the thing in question; (4) explanation is by way of relating tendencies to natures, rather than through deriving tendencies from generalizations.

(1) For Marx, physical necessity pertains primarily to the developmental life of an individual. Indeed, when I said something about the explication of 'it is physically necessary that if p, then q', I did not assume that I was dealing with explicit or implied generalizations. For Marx p and q would be replaced by propositions about individuals, about the unfolding of the life history of a thing. For Marx, nomologicity and physical necessity are not related to generalizations over individuals or particulars in the sorts of ways supposed by the empiricist tradition, but rather are firmly rooted in the idea of the development of an individual. In this spirit, Marx mentions 'the general law of *capitalist* accumulation', 'the law of value', 'the law of the tendency of the falling rate of profit', all of which are laws of restricted application, to the life of a *single* individual of its kind. Thus, the validity of the law is restricted by the lifetime of that individual. As Lukacs says in 'What is Orthodox Marxism?', Marx's method 'is in its innermost essence, historical'. What this means here is that his scientific investigation is set to uncover the laws of the physically necessary motion of a particular thing (for example capitalism as an individual mode of production among others), and not to find general laws which are supposed to apply without any restrictions whatsoever. If the object of study is the particular mode of production, capitalism, then the study involves studying its necessary developmental history, and not trying to produce generalizations which would apply without limitation *across* all modes of production. Of course, if one does study the particular mode of production, capitalism, one will have arrived at an understanding of a *plurality* of societies, at least insofar as they are capitalist. But the point remains: the interest is in arriving at the laws of necessary motion of a particular socio-economic structure, not in

arriving at the laws of motion of *all* kinds of structures. Upon these two different conceptions of scientific enquiry rest two different conceptions of the aims of scientific practice, the former typically a Marxian one, the latter characteristic of the empiricist philosophy of science. Because studying a mode of production involves coming to understand the developmental life of an individual, it bears some resemblance to learning about the biography of a person. In both cases, the course of an individual's life is traced. The biography of a person chronicles events that arise both because of the intrinsic character of the person and because of the accidental vicissitudes and vagaries that life throws in the path of the person. If we could imagine a biography that reported about a person's life *only* insofar as its course arose from or was related to what that person was himself, then the parallel between writing a biography of a person and producing a scientific study of a mode of production would be even closer.

So far, then, I have wedded Marx to the idea that the task of science is to uncover the workings of each particular mode of production. Since a mode of production can be exemplified in a plurality of historical societies separated both in time and space, and since more than one mode of production can coexist in a single, historical society, modes of production are, unlike persons, and unlike historical societies, abstract objects, not concrete ones. Thus, an historical society, for example Russia in 1916, might have internally different tendencies which arise from the various modes of production which can be found there in varying degrees. This presupposes, of course, the viability of the notion of a mode of production, and the possibility of some sort of criteria by which to individuate modes of production. I cannot defend either presupposition here. But I would like to remark on the way in which such a conception could deal with the problem of transitional modes of production. It might be said, as Ernest Mandel does for example, that the 'transitional' mode of production in Eastern Europe and the Soviet Union is a 'hybrid', embodying both the law of value and planning. If this were so, an understanding of a transitional mode of production would produce no special problems; one would *more or less* have understood the hybrid, or at least have the conceptual apparatus to do so, once one understood the capitalist and socialist modes of production. On the other hand, it might be said – and this seems to be far more plausible – that this transitional mode of production is a mode of production in its own right, with its own particular laws of motion. If so, then the problem of understanding the transition (from capitalism to socialism) is the problem of understanding an additional mode of production, with its own 'nature' and necessary developments. This is not to say that it would be plausible for *every* historical transition period, but rather for this particular transition.

(2) Such necessary development or dependence is tendential rather than actual. Marx's claims about necessary development or dependence are at a level of abstraction which is not immediate, not at the level of manifest, concrete reality. Marx did not deny that there are causally sufficient conditions for everything that occurs, but he would deny that it was the task of science to formulate laws which encapsulate all these complicated and often irrelevant, from the point of view of science, conditions which might, jointly, be sufficient for the actual occurrence of the phenomenon under investigation. From the point of view of a science, some of the things which happen to the individual it may be studying are accidental, even though they are caused to occur, and hence it may be unnecessary to consider the cause which produce such (what are from its point of view) accidents or to include reference to them in the formulation of laws. In addition to 'it is physically necessary that', there is also the operator 'it is accidental that', but the existence of the latter does not commit science to the recognition of indeterminism.

'Tendential' is not meant in a statistical sense, for such tendencies might rarely or never manifest themselves. Hence, such laws cannot be read as predictions or claims about the actual or probable occurrence of events in the life of the individual, although clearly they can be used in a *mediated* manner to comprehend or understand the individual. Necessity pertains not to actual occurrences, but to the *tendencies* inherent in things, how they are represented as behaving when studied at a certain level of abstraction at which both non-essential impediments to those tendencies and tendencies which pull in an opposite direction are disregarded. Thus, in Marx's most famous nomological pronouncement about capitalism: 'The law of the tendency of the rate of profit to fall', which he can show follows 'with logical necessity', 'from the nature of the capitalist mode of production'.[55] What the law does is to describe a tendency which arises 'from the nature of the capitalist mode of production', from its essence, and such a tendency can be blocked, impeded, thwarted or indeed encouraged or exacerbated, by other factors which may themselves be tendencies. Elsewhere, in *Capital* Volume I, he speaks of the 'historical tendency of capitalist accumulation', and again in Volume III of Capital:

> Such a general rate of surplus-value – viewed as a tendency, like all other economic laws – has been assumed by us for the sake of theoretical simplification. But in reality it is an actual premise of the capitalist mode of production, although it is more or less obstructed by practical frictions causing more or less considerable local differences ... But in theory it is assumed that the laws of capitalist production operate in their pure form. In reality, there exists only approximation; but, this approximation is the greater, the more developed the capitalist mode of production and the less it is adulterated and amalgamated with survivals of former economic conditions.[56]

If the tendencies are thwarted, they may not become actualized at all, or only in a vastly altered form, or only after a long delay. Similarly, if they are encouraged or heightened, they may become actual earlier. This explains the idea advanced by many Marxists that revolutionary activity 'speeds up' a result which would, in any case, necessarily occur. A problem which has generally bedevilled Marxist theorists is that of how Marxism as a science and as a practice could be made compatible. For us, this whole discussion has raged around a pseudo-problem. These theorists have either explicitly or implicitly retained the notion of necessity in their understanding of causal law and hence of the nature of science. Empiricists attempted to make science and human freedom 'compatible' by extruding any idea of necessity from their analyses of causation; a similar move was not open to these Marxist theorists. Now, if what is taken to be necessary for Marx are *actual* occurrences, science would genuinely be incompatible with human freedom. But, on the other hand, if what is physically necessary about the life history of a thing is only that it has a *tendency* to develop in certain ways, then one can see the relevance of revolutionary practice in *using* scientific results, *true ones*, to impede, block, or hasten and develop the actual manifestation of those physically necessary tendencies.

Failure to understand the 'tendential' nature of Marx's conception of necessary development has given rise to countless misunderstandings of his work. For example, Marx calls the increasing misery of the proletariat 'the absolute general law of capitalist accumulation'. It is useless to try to immediately verify or falsify the law by comparing it with actual social facts as they present themselves. Marx adds, after the statement of the law: 'Like all other laws it is modified in its working by many circumstances, the analysis of which does not concern us here.'[57] Since laws as they describe the nomic behaviour of individuals do not operate at the level of the actual, but rather at the level of the tendential, which may or may not become manifest, predictions cannot be immediately made from the statement of laws. Such laws can be *true* even if the tendencies of which they speak do not become manifest.

(3) Marx says, as quoted earlier, that 'the law of the tendency of the rate of profit to fall' follows 'from the nature of capitalist development'. That is, tendencies follow with physical necessity from the nature or constitution of a thing. For Marx, unlike Hegel, the dynamic tendencies or movements of things occur at least in part because of the contradictions which are essential to them, ineradicably part of their nature. This is implicit or explicit in just about everything that Marx writes, for he makes it clear that something like capitalism develops necessarily through the presence within it of its essential contradictions. In the case of a mode of production at least, Marx frequently insists that the essence of a thing is relational, embodying contradictions, necessary conflicts and oppositions. For each case, the scientific task is

to demonstrate how the contradictory features of the nature of a thing force it to tend to move – no external appeal is necessary. As indicated earlier, both history and nature move for Hegel, but only because they are the motions of another, the expressions of oppositions that are not ultimately their own. Because for Marx oppositions are 'real and autonomous', and pertain to a thing's nature or essence, the necessary tendencies of a thing are real and inescapable.

Thus, in the schema I used earlier, 'it is physically necessary that if p, then q', I take it that the antecedent proposition is about the nature or essential constitution of a thing, and q is about some developmental tendency in the life history of that individual. It is, then, physically necessary that something with a certain structure or composition tends to act, behave, or develop in certain sorts of way. Lenin's pamphlet, *Imperialism: The Highest Stage of Capitalism*, is an example of an attempt to discover and describe such physical necessities that flow from the nature of capitalism. Similarly, someone who asserted that capitalism is necessarily racist or sexist would be advancing the same sort of claim. It is not that capitalist societies are always and everywhere racist or sexist, but rather that there is an underlying tendency toward the development of these phenomena which follows with physical necessity from the nature of capitalist (but not only) society itself.[58]

Many Marxists have been wary of any reading of Marx which attributes to him a theory of 'essential' structure, perhaps because of Marx's own critical remarks about any theory of human nature or essence. However, there is no doubt that Marx spoke in this way, for example.'the essence of bourgeois society consists precisely in this, that *a priori* there is no conscious social regulation of production',[59] and perhaps enough has already been said about how to understand such claims about a thing's essence to dispel historical caution about natures or essences. Marx, as is known, contrasted a theory of human nature with a relational understanding of man, by which man is the 'sum' of the social relations into which he enters. There is nothing 'un-relational' about the natures or essences of modes of production that we have in mind; the natures or essences of a mode of production which ground nomologically its development are themselves 'relational' – the natures consist, *inter alia*, of a set of relations between social classes or groups.

What is the relationship between a thing and its nature or essential structure? Is it only physically necessary that capitalism has the sort of class structure it has? Or have we here genuine examples of logical necessity? There are many 'compositional' claims in Marx's writings which he seems to have thought were *necessary* in some sense. Take, for example, the pair, wage labour and capital; Marx says: 'Thus capital presupposes wage labour; wage labour presupposes capital. They reciprocally condition the existence of each other.'[60] The whole, capitalism, is necessarily composed of wage labour and capital; each part, wage labour for example, necessarily presupposes the other part, capital, and *vice versa* ('they reciprocally condition the existence of each other'). This is a claim of necessary composition (of a whole) or necessary interdependence (and opposition) of its parts. Another example occurs in *A Contribution to the Critique of Political Economy*, in which Marx speaks of the 'simultaneous' identity of sale and purchase: 'a sale is simultaneously its opposite, a purchase, and *vice versa*'.[61] The particular point Marx is making is that each exchange is *necessarily* composed of a sale and a purchase, and that the sale necessarily presupposes a purchase, and *vice versa*. Earlier, I quoted Marx's remark from *The Economic and Philosophical Manuscripts of 1844* that society was 'the consummated oneness in substance of man and nature', which seems like a claim for necessary composition, viz. that society is necessarily composed of, or presupposes, both man and nature. Often, Marx uses the word 'unity' rather than 'identity' to mark off these claims of necessary composition or structure, as he does for example in *The German Ideology*, when he says that the 'unity of man with nature' has always existed in industry . . .'[62]

These claims of necessary structure or composition are, at least sometimes, claims not of physical necessity but of logical necessity. This seems patently true with the example of sale and purchase, for it seems that in every logically possible world in which there is a sale it is related to a complementary purchase. Suppose one asks: is it merely a physical necessity that capitalism developed the class structure of wage labour and capital that it does have? Is there a possible world in which capitalism existed without developing that structure? I think that there is no such possible world, and hence that it is true in all possible worlds in which capitalism exists that capitalism developed its class structure of wage labour and capital. Of course, there is a logically possible world in which capitalism failed to exist at all, just as there is a possible world in which there is no element with the atomic number 79. The world might (logically speaking) have come to an end in 1400 A.D. There is a logically possible world in which some other mode of production, perhaps bearing some similarities to capitalism, replaced feudalism across Europe. Merchant capital, where we find capital but no wage labour, might, logically speaking, never have developed into capitalism proper. Thus, essentialism is compatible with Marx's historical understanding. It is not necessary that capitalism existed at all, and it is not necessary that capitalism continues to exist. It is not necessary that there be the individual mode of production, capitalism. What is logically necessary is not capitalism but that, for as long as that individual mode of production does exist, it has the same essential class structure, in however a modified or unmanifested form. Since this is what is true about capitalism in all possible worlds in which it exists, what is not possible is that there be a world in which that *particular* mode of production, capitalism, existed without its essential class structure. If this is correct, then perhaps it explains what is wrong with one form of reformism. If class structure, and the opposition of these classes, were not essential to capitalism, then presumably capitalism could be modified or reformed in acceptable ways. It is because class division and opposition are essential to capitalism that this reform is not possible.

Thus, when Marx says that wage labour presupposes capital and *vice versa*, he is making a logically necessary claim about the essential class structure of capitalist society. If these claims about essences are true in all possible worlds, there is no doubt that they are knowable only *a posteriori*. Knowledge of the essential structure of a thing, as well as knowledge of its necessary developmental history, is the fruit of scientific enquiry, not *a priori* philosophical speculation. This epistemological point applies then, both to physical necessities of development and logical necessities of essential structure.

Earlier, I mentioned the examples of imperialism and monopoly and racism and sexism as physically necessary developmental tendencies which arise from the nature of capitalism. In this section, I have spoken of the wage labour and capital class structure of capitalism as logically necessary to capitalism (that is in any *possible* world in which capitalism exists, it has that structure). What about the tendency of the rate of profit to fall? Marx asserts, in Volume III of *Capital*, that such a tendency follows with 'logical necessity' from the nature of capital, and so *a fortiori* this must be true of such phenomena as exploitation, capital accumulation, and the growth of the organic composition of capital as well. To think this issue through properly entails coming to a very sophisticated and detailed understanding of *Capital*, in order to see what does genuinely follow *deductively* from the analysis of the class relations and the law of value which are implicit in the notion of a commodity with which Marx begins, and what follows only with additional empirical assumptions.

Thus, if an example of 'it is physically necessary that if *p*, then *q*' is something like 'it is physically necessary that, given the analysis of the commodity and what that implies for the law of value and the essential class relations of capitalism, then capitalism will have a tendency to develop monopolies', we can say the following. The whole conditional assertion is physically necessary. The antecedent of the conditional is logically necessary in the weak sense in which, in every possible world in which commodities exist, their existence entails the same essential class structure of wage labour and capital and the operation of the law of value however modified or obscured from casual observation. Both the whole conditional assertion, as well as the fact that the antecedent is itself weakly logically necessary, are only knowable *a posteriori*, through scientific enquiry.

I have already claimed that, for Marx, physical necessity and nomologicity were not related to generalizations over individuals in the sorts of ways supposed by the empiricist tradition, but rather are firmly rooted in the idea of the development of an individual. Perhaps the introduction of talk about essences can give some purchase on why this might be so.

If I claim that it is physically necessary for this particular acorn to grow into an oak tree, this physically necessary tendency statement *is* related in an obvious way to a generalization – it is physically necessary that all acorns grow into oak trees. This is because all acorns share a generic nature or essence – whatever structure is essential to this acorn being just what it is is similarly essential to any acorn whatever. To tell the story of the intrinsic unfolding of the life of this acorn is to tell exactly the same story as would be told about any other acorn. But, unlike acorns, modes of production have individual essences which they do not share with any other mode of production. It is physically necessary that, if anything has the same nature as this acorn, it grows into an oak too. But if any other mode of production had the same essential structure as capitalism, it just *would be* capitalism. Thus, physically necessary statements about modes of production do not imply or sustain generalizations in the same way as do physically necessary statements about acorns.

(4) For Marx, the criteria for a good explanation centre upon relating the tendencies of a thing to its essential nature or structure, rather than deriving statements of tendencies from generalizations, as an empiricist account of explanation might suggest. Now, Marx certainly does not rule out that one can make legitimate generalizations across individuals, types of modes of production, etc., but he does not think that such generalizations amount to more than *descriptions*. They do not, for Marx, have the *force* of a *law* (even though he does sometimes call them 'laws'), and this on the grounds that such generalizations lack the explanatory force associated with a law of science which is about the development of an individual. For Marx, generality and explanatory force tend to run in opposite directions.

Marx discusses the role of generalization at several points, but perhaps the most extensive treatment occurs in the

'Introduction to the *Grundrisse*'. It is worthwhile quoting from it:

> Thus when we speak of production, we always have in mind production at a definite stage of social development, production by individuals in a society ... All periods of production, however, have certain features in common: they have certain common categories. *Production in general* is an abstraction, insofar as it actually emphasizes and defines the common aspects and thus avoids repetition. ... [However] it is precisely their divergence from the general and common features *which constitutes their development* [my emphasis – DHR]. It is necessary to distinguish those definitions which apply to production in general, in order not to overlook the essential differences existing despite the unity that follows from the very fact that the subject, mankind, and the object, nature, are the same ...

> ... [with reference to Adam Smith's generalization about conditions which promote production] to give this, which in Smith's work has its value as an *apercu*, to give it scientific significance, research into the *degree of productivity* at various periods in the development of individual nations would have to be conducted.[63]

Even when Marx does refer to such 'general definitions' elsewhere as 'natural laws' – for example, when he says that the '*necessity* of the *distribution* of social labour in definite proportions cannot possibly be done away with by a *particular* form of social production ... no natural laws can be done away with'[64] – the point about their explanatory inadequacy, which arises from their generality, remains the same. 'There are categories which are common to all stages of production, and which are established by reasoning as general categories; the so-called *general conditions* of all and any production, however, are nothing but abstract conceptions which do not define any of the actual historical stages of production.'[65] Thus, these 'general definitions' have little explanatory value. It is the ways in which modes of production are specific or unique or individual that 'constitute their development', and hence explanation of that development cannot rely on such generalizations, but rather only on an understanding of the particular mode of production under study. Moreover, according to Marx, such generalizations are constantly in danger of being misused by ideologists and apologists of the present, to 'prove the eternity and harmony of existing social relations'.

This view of the nature of necessity, law and explanation permits us to understand Marx's caution in espousing any simplistic version of historical materialism that is meant to apply to the succession of modes of production. As already indicated, Marx speaks of laws of a particular mode of production. In fact, on several occasions he expressed reservations about speaking of a general law which governed the succession of modes of production. This can perhaps be most clearly seen in two letters in which he discussed Russia and the supposed need for specifically capitalist development there. In an 1877 letter to Mikhailovsky:

> Now what application to Russia could my critic make of this historical sketch? Only this: if Russia is tending to become a capitalist nation after the example of West European countries . . . she will not succeed without having first transformed a good part of her peasants into proletarians; and after that, once taken to the bosom of the capitalist regime, she will experience its pitiless laws like other profane peoples. That is all. But that is too little for my critic. He feels he must metamorphose my historical sketch of the genesis of capitalism in Western Europe into a historico-philosophic theory of the general path every people is fated to tread, whatever the historical circumstances in which it finds itself . . .

> Thus events strikingly analogous but taking place in different historical surroundings led to totally different results. By studying each of these forms of evolution separately and then comparing them one can easily find the clue to this phenomenon, but one will never arrive there by using as one's master key a general historico-philosophical theory, the supreme virtue of which consists in being supra-historical.

Then, in an 1881 letter to Vera Zassoulitch:

> If capitalist production must establish its reign in Russia, the great majority of Russian people . . . must be converted into wage earners, and consequently expropriated by the preliminary abolition of its communist property. But in any case the western precedent would not prove anything at all concerning the 'historical fatality' of this process.[66]

In these letters Marx insists that *if* 'Russia is tending to become a capitalist nation', '*if* capitalist production must establish its reign in Russia', then the necessary tendencies, the 'pitiless laws' of capitalism will apply. But there are no laws across epochs which dictate that Russia must become capitalist. In the letter to Mikhailovsky, Marx *denies* by way of the example of the Roman proletarians that it is necessary that all societies develop production 'in order that it may ultimately arrive at the form of economy which ensures, together with the greatest expansion of the productive powers of social labour, the most complete development of man.' No law dictates that this is the course of necessary development, for laws apply to a particular mode of production, and not across modes of production. I do not claim that nothing in Marx suggests any view other than this one. There are certainly occasions, and one can think especially of some of his assertions in the Preface to *A Contribution to the Critique of Political Economy*, where Marx does seem to be propounding some sort of trans-historical laws about social development. 'No social order is ever destroyed before all the productive forces for which it is sufficient have been developed . . . '[67] But one does not need to construe such statements as laws which provide explanatory force in coming to understand the change, development, and revolution that comes to modes of production. Rather, such statements are summaries, descriptive generalizations about the path all (or some) societies have hitherto taken. But, in each case, in understanding why a particular mode of production has taken such a path, one does not cite the generalization but investigates the law of development of *that* particular mode of production. I do not say that generalizations such as that concerning the contradiction between the forces and relations of production acting as the 'dynamic' of historical change are not true. Rather, I claim that they can be treated as generalizations which as such have no independent nomic force. In those specific cases where the contradiction between the forces and relations of production does lead to social revolution, citing the contradiction does have explanatory force. The generalization, even if true, simply summarizes the particular, specific explanations of each instance. Nomologicity relates to the particular; the generalization summarizes explanatory results fully achieved in particular cases. Construing these trans-historical truths in such a fashion fits in well with what Marx elsewhere had to say about his historical method:

> Viewed apart from real history, these abstractions have in themselves no value whatsoever. They can only serve to facilitate the arrangement of historical material, to indicate the sequence of its separate strata. But they by no means afford a recipe or schema, as does philosophy, for neatly trimming the epochs of history.[68]

This, then, completes the four related points about Marx's conception of physical necessity that I undertook to discuss. Such a conception also has clear implications for Marx's view of science. First, let me say that I offer the account as Marx's view on the scientific study of society, for the role of explanation and generalization that I have here sketched surely could not be similarly plausible in its entirety in the natural sciences. I think that slogans such as 'the methods of the natural and social sciences are the same' or 'the methods of the natural and social sciences are different' are each far too unrefined to be anything like the truth. They must be similar in some respects and different in others. I think Marx's views on necessity, structure, and tendencies would equally well apply to the natural and social sciences; clearly, his views on generalization and explanation would not.

Because for Marx science itself deals with the necessary developmental tendencies inherent in things, science therefore deals with things in necessary connection and motion. That is, science itself is dialectical, and hence needs no external dialectical supplementation as it did with Hegel. Indeed, what for Hegel was a contrast between undialectical science and dialectical philosophy becomes for Marx a distinction between undialectical ideology or apology – which 'eternalizes' things by divorcing them from movement – and dialectical science. For Marx, it is one of the hallmarks of ideology that it performs this function that Hegel had assigned to science: thus, in criticism of those who are misled by generalizations, and who are therefore accustomed to conclude that 'capital is a universal and eternal relation given by nature, that is provided one omits precisely the specific factors . . . ',[69] Marx poses the alternative of a science which sets all things in their proper historical setting and delimitation, and a science moreover whose task it is to investigate the physically necessary consequences that flow from the structure and composition of those historically delimited individuals. This is an alternative which Trotsky echoes in his understanding of what he must do in recounting the history of the Russian revolution:

> a scientific conscientiousness . . . seeks support in an honest study of the facts, a determination of their real connections, an exposure of the causal laws of their movement. That is the only possible historical objectivism, and moreover it is amply sufficient, for it is verified and attested not by the good intentions of the historian, for which only he can vouch, but by the natural laws revealed by him of the historic process itself.[70]

Notes

1   For such an interpretation, see for example, Alexandre Kojéve, *Introduction to the Reading of Hegel*, Allan Bloom (ed.) (New York 1969).

2   Hegel, *The Logic of Hegel*, William Wallace (tr.) from *The Encyclopaedia of the Philosophical Sciences* (Oxford 1972), pp. 194, 219.

3   Hegel, *The Phenomenology of Mind*, J. B. Baillie (tr.) (London, 1966), Preface, p. 112.

4   Hegel, *The Logic of Hegel*, pp. 213–14.

5   *Ibid.* p. 147.

6   *Ibid.* p. 150.

7   *Ibid.* pp. 150–1.

8   *Ibid.* pp. 19–20.

9   Hegel, *The Phenomenology of Mind*, pp. 111–12.

10 Hegel, *The Logic of Hegel*, p. 144.

11 Hegel, *The Philosophy of Nature*, A. V. Miller (tr.) from *The Encyclopaedia of the Philosophical Sciences* (Oxford 1970), p. 6.

12 *Ibid.* p. 10.

13 *Ibid.* p. 11.

14 First quote is from *ibid.* p. 10; the second from Hegel, *The Logic*, p. 22.

15 Hegel, *The Philosophy of Nature*, p. 10.

16 *Ibid.* p. 6.

17 *Ibid.* p. 11.

18 *Ibid.* p. 8.

19 Hegel, *The Phenomenology of Mind*, p. 789.

20 Hegel, *The Logic of Hegel*, Introduction, p. 20.

21 *Ibid.* p. 22.

22 Hegel, *The Phenomenology of Mind*, p. 112.

23 Hegel, *The Philosophy of Nature*, p. 20.

24 G. Lukacs, *The Young Hegel* (London 1975), p. 542.

25 *Ibid.* p. 546.

26 *Ibid.* p. 547.

27 These quotations are all taken from the section on production and consumption in Marx's discussion of method in 'Introduction to the *Grundrisse*'. Subsequent quotations on their relation are taken from the same discussion unless otherwise indicated. See either Karl Marx, *A Contribution to the Critique of Political Economy*, Maurice Dobb (ed.) (London 1971) pp. 195–9; or T. Carver, *Karl Marx: Texts on Method* (Oxford 1975), pp. 58–64.

28 Karl Marx, *Wage-Labour and Capital* (Moscow 1970), p. 31.

29 Karl Marx, *Capital*, I. (Moscow 1965), p. 763.

30 Karl Marx, 'Afterword to the second German edition', *Capital*, I. (Moscow 1965), pp. 19–20.

31 See Bertell Ollman, *Alienation* (Cambridge 1971).

32 Karl Marx, *The Economic and Philosophical Manuscripts of 1844* (Moscow 1967), pp. 97, 102.

33 It now seems to me that I did not sufficiently appreciate Lukacs' qualification of the identity of subject and object as applicable only to the social realm in my discussion of Lukacs in *Marxism and Materialism: A Study in Marxist Theory of Knowledge* (Hassocks 1977).

34 G. Lukacs, *History and Class Consciousness* (London 1971), p. 206.

35 *Ibid*. p. 207.

36 G. Lukacs, *The Young Hegel*, p. 270.

37 *Ibid*. p. 271.

38 *Ibid*. p. 514.

39 Karl Marx, *Capital*, I, p. 74.

40 See for example Marx's discussion of Hegel's *The Phenomenology of Mind* in *The Economic and Philosophic Manuscripts of 1844*, in the manuscript entitled (in the Progress Publishers edition) 'Critique of the Hegelian dialectic, and philosophy as a whole'.

41 Lucio Colletti, *Marxism and Hegel* (London 1973), pp. 7–27.

42 *Ibid*. p. 14.

43 *Ibid*. p. 17.

44 I carefully avoid such terms as 'conceptual necessity'. In this paper, I have little to say about logical necessity, other than insisting on distinguishing it from natural necessity. That distinction is between what is true in all possible worlds, and what is true in some proper subset of those worlds, a subset which includes more than the actual world. But I do not subscribe to the thesis that all such logical necessities arise from meanings, conventions, definitions, stipulations, or concepts; I do not think that '*de dicto*' marks in a useful way any kind of necessity, unless it is merely one of the scope of the modal operator.

45 See Guy Robinson, 'Nature and necessity' in *The Royal Institute of Philosophy Lectures* 1974–5, for the idea of a nomological truth based on (Aristotelian) potentialities and powers of things. See especially pp. 207–208.

46 See my book, *Marxism and Materialism*, ch. 2, for some remarks on Feuerbach's views on *de re* physical necessity.

47 This point is mentioned by Milton Fisk, *Nature and Necessity* (Bloomington 1973), p. 27.

48 M. R. Ayers, *The Refutation of Determinism* (London 1968). See especially pp. 68–101, from which all subsequent quotes from the book are taken.

49 These attempts can be found in David Lewis, 'Causation', *Journal of Philosophy*, 70 (1973), pp. 556–67, and reprinted in Ernest Sosa (ed.), *Causation and Conditionals* (Oxford 1975), pp. 180–91, and in Karl Popper, *The Logic of Scientific Discovery* (London 1972), pp. 420–41.

50 For a critical discussion of Popper's 'definition' of physical necessity, see W. Suchting, 'Popper's revised definition of natural necessity', *British Journal for the Philosophy of Science*, XX (1969), pp. 349–52, and G. C. Nerlich and W. A. Suchting, 'Popper on law and natural necessity', *British Journal for the Philosophy of Science*, XVIII (1967), pp. 233–5.

51 J. L. Mackie, *The Cement of the Universe* (Oxford 1974), pp. 212–13.

52 J. L. Mackie, *Truth, Probability and Paradox* (Oxford 1973), pp. 89–90, and see Lewis' reply in *Counterfactuals* (Oxford 1973), pp. 84–95.

53 Milton Fisk, 'Are there necessary connections in nature?', *Philosophy of Science*, XXXVII (1970), pp. 385–404. All quotations are taken from p. 388.

54 Colin McGinn, 'A note on the essence of natural kinds', *Analysis*, 35.6 (June 1975), pp. 177–83. All quotations are from pp. 179–81.

55 Karl Marx, *Capital*, III (Moscow 1966), p. 213.

56 *Ibid.* p. 175.

57 Karl Marx, *Capital*, I, p. 644, discussed by Paul Sweezy in *The Theory of Capitalist Development* (New York 1968), p. 19. Chapter 1 of Sweezy's book contains a useful if elementary discussion of Marx's method.

58 There have been several attempts to ground physical necessity on the natures of things. I quoted approvingly in note 45 Guy Robinson's remarks on this. Milton Fisk, in *Nature and Necessity* and Roy Bhaskar, *A Realist Theory of Science* (Leeds 1975 and Hassocks 1978), have produced attempts to do this. These attempts do not by-pass the sorts of problems discussed by Lewis or Popper, since one still needs to know the truth-conditions for statements which assert that something has such-and-such a nature, or acts or behaves in certain ways by nature.

59 Marx, Letter to Kugelmann, 11 July 1868, in Marx and Engels, *Selected Correspondence* (Moscow).

60 Karl Marx, *Wage-Labour and Capital*, p. 31.

61 Karl Marx, *A Contribution to the Critique of Political Economy*, p. 94.

62 Karl Marx, *The German Ideology* (Moscow 1968), p. 58.

63 Karl Marx, 'Introduction to the *Grundrisse*', Maurice Dobb (ed.), pp. 189–91.

64 Karl Marx, *Letters to Dr. Kugelmann*, p. 251.

65 Karl Marx, 'Introduction to the *Grundrisse*', p. 193.

66 Both letters are quoted in David McLellan, *The Thought of Karl Marx*, (London 1971), pp. 135–7. Marx is considering only tendencies 'internal' to Russian society itself. Scott Meikle has pointed out to me that if one considers wider tendencies, for example the tendency of the world market to pull societies into its international orbit, one can speak of tendencies for Russia to become capitalist, tendencies which were happily blocked. Like Marx, I ignore here these tendencies and focus only on the tendency inherent in the society itself, in abstracted isolation from the world perspective.

67 Karl Marx, 'Preface to A *Contribution to the Critique of Political Economy*', p. 21
68 Karl Marx, *The German Ideology* (Moscow 1968), pp. 38–9.
69 Karl Marx, 'Introduction to the *Grundrisse*', p. 190.
70 Leon Trotsky, *The History of the Russian Revolution*, I. (London 1967), p. 19.

3 *Dialectics and Labour*

CHRIS ARTHUR

Marx and Hegel

NOTHING in Marxist philosophy is more obscure than the precise relation of Marx to Hegel on the question of the dialectic. In his *Capital* Marx declares enigmatically:

> The mystification which dialectic suffers in Hegel's hands, by no means prevents him from being the first to present its general form of working. ... With him it is standing on its head. It must be turned right side up again, if you would discover the rational kernel within the mystical shell.[1]

What does this mean? Attempts to produce a materialist dialectic, 'right side up', through some, more or less formal, transformation of the general categories of Hegel's *Logic*, prove singularly unrewarding. More fruitful than this may be a close examination of Marx's substantive scientific work, directed towards the identification of methods, arguments, and concepts, that may be characterized as dialectical. In part, this paper takes up the question of Marx's acknowledged debt to Hegel's *Logic* in the chapter on value in *Capital*[2] – with particular reference to the modalities of labour.

The assumption of many of Marx's critics is that the influence of Hegel must be pernicious, and is likely to produce metaphysical, rather than scientific, modes of argument. However, since Marx himself was a trenchant critic of Idealism, and yet aware that this dialectical method was prefigured in Hegel, it is possible that he was capable of utilizing Hegel's work to the extent that was compatible with rejection of Hegelian 'mystification'. My argument will show that, while Marx's theory of value reflects certain themes in Hegel's philosophy, the analysis is firmly grounded in material reality and is not open to the objections that Marx himself propounded against philosophical speculation.

In the 1873 edition of *Capital* Marx points out that he criticized the mystifying side of the Hegelian dialectic nearly thirty years before.[3] The reference here must be to *The Holy Family* of 1845. What was the character of this criticism?

The Mystery of Speculative Construction

Under the above heading Marx presents the following caricature of idealist method in terms of the notion of 'fruit'. If from real apples, pears, oranges and so on, is formed the general idea 'Fruit', then the speculative philosopher takes this abstract idea to be a self-sufficient entity which is indeed the true essence or 'substance' of the apple, pear, etc. The appearance of *diversity* in the manifestations of this unitary 'substance' seems a problem. However, the speculative philosopher explains that this diversity arises because '*the* fruit' is not dead, undifferentiated, static, but a living, self-differentiating, moving essence: '*the* Fruit' presents itself, now as an apple, now as a pear – the differences between fruits are *self-differentiations* of '*the* Fruit'. The unity grasped in this concept is not empty, it is oneness as allness, as the 'totality' of an organically linked series of members, through each of which '*the* Fruit' develops its existence more explicitly until, in the summary of all fruits, it is a living unity.[4]

Marx comments on this by saying that the speculative philosopher presents the activity of thought (his *own* activity) in passing from the notion of apple to that of pear, as the 'self-activity' of the absolute subject – in this case '*the* Fruit'. 'This operation is called comprehending *Substance* as *Subject*', says Marx, and it 'constitutes the essential character of Hegel's method'.[5]

In *Capital* Marx sums up his view again by charging Hegel with presenting 'the process of thinking', under the name of 'the Idea', as an independent subject, as 'the *demiurgos* of the real world'.[6]

Marx's 'Hegelian Construction'

It has been argued by Stanley Moore that Marx uses the same idealist method in his theory of value. Moore claims to discover a parallelism between the positions identified and criticized by Marx as Hegelian in 1845 and Marx's use of the concept 'abstract labour' in the first chapter of *Capital* (1867):

(1) Searching for a common property in terms of which quantities of different commodities can be equated for exchange, Marx forms the idea of abstract labour.
(2) He then concludes that this idea of abstract labour, as an entity existing outside him, is the essence or substance of the exchange values of the different commodities.
(3) Why then, he asks, does this substance manifest itself sometimes in one kind of commodity, sometimes in another? Why this appearance of diversity?
(4) Because, he answers, abstract labour is not static, undifferentiated, dead—but dynamic, self-differentiated, alive. The values of different commodities are externalizations of one labour process, the productive activity of society as a whole.[7]

On Moore's account, then, we might conclude that Marx reads into the facts of commodity exchange the same kind of 'speculative construction' that he earlier rejected.

Now Marx was always most punctilious in *Capital* about giving credit to such previous political economists who had first formulated certain ideas – no matter how obscurely. It is worth paying attention, therefore, when Marx makes his solitary claim to originality in the opening chapter. The point that labour has a two-fold nature, 'abstract' and 'concrete' (for, 'in so far as it finds expression in value, it does not possess the same characteristics that belong to it as a creator of use-values'), is, he says, the 'pivot on which a clear comprehension of Political Economy turns'. 'I was the first', he claims, 'to point out and to examine critically this two-fold nature of the labour contained in commodities'.[8] The development of the concept of 'abstract labour' was regarded by Marx as a key scientific achievement – yet it is just this concept which Moore regards as speculative. Below I shall elucidate the character of this concept of 'abstract labour' and offer a view of it different from that propounded by Stanley Moore in the précis quoted above. First, however, it is necessary to develop an overall view of the modalities of labour, the nature of commodity exchange, and the relations involved.

Productive Forces and Production Relations
Our treatment will follow the distinction made by Marx in his

famous 1859 *Preface* where he says that, at a certain stage of development, there correspond to men's powers of production, or productive forces, certain relations of production, the sum total of which forms the economic structure of society.[9] The point of this is to bring out systematically the nature of the different realms to which Marx implicitly refers labour in its concrete useful form, on the one hand, and labour taken up as abstract in value, on the other.

First labour-power will be analysed as a *force of production*, and in the process it will be argued that in a developed industrial economy social labour, as a productive force, has a fluidity in its forms of appearance which gives a material basis to a characterization of it as concretely universal.

However, the social productive forces (the primary mediation of man with nature) only operate within certain *relations of production* (second order mediations governing the appropriation of the produce socially). It will be argued that in commodity production labour is not immediately social, but private, and therefore that the sociality of labour in the process of commodity production is realized, and recognized, in commodity exchange relations only by the mediation of value.

Value is a relation of production. Its substance – abstract labour – must thus be understood as a form of existence of labour specific to commodity production (whereas the concrete forms of labour exist whatever social relations mediate production – just as a body always has mass but only has weight in a gravitational field). I go on to investigate the complex relations between the concrete universality of social labour at the level of the production of use-values and its incorporation as an abstract unity in the sphere of value relations. This will make possible an assessment of the charge that an idealist construction is involved. At the conclusion it will be suggested that Marx's dialectical analysis of the commodity differs from Hegel's *Logic* in being immanently critical of its object.

Labour as a Productive Force
Now to some remarks Marx makes about labour as a productive force. It should be stressed that in this discussion

there is no need to refer to his value theory: that is dealt with later in the discussion of commodity relations.

Consider the point Marx makes about two qualitatively different kinds of labour – tailoring and weaving:

> There are, however, states of society in which one and the same man does tailoring and weaving alternately, in which case these two forms of labour are mere modifications of the labour of the same individual, and no special and fixed functions of different persons, just as the coat which our tailor makes one day, and the trousers which he makes another day, imply only a variation in the labour of one and the same individual. Moreover, we see at a glance that, in our capitalist society, a given portion of human labour is in accordance with the varying demand, at one time supplied in the form of tailoring, at another in the form of weaving. This change may possibly not take place without friction, but take place it must.
>
> Productive activity, if we leave out of sight its special form, viz. the useful character of the labour, is nothing but the expenditure of human labour power. Tailoring and weaving, though qualitatively different productive activities, are each a productive expenditure of human brains, nerves, and muscles, and in this sense are human labour. They are but two different modes of expending human labour-power.[10]

The 'productive expenditure of human brains, nerves and muscles' naturally takes various forms, but it is a presupposition of any economic analysis that these various manifestations of the expenditure of labour-power may be considered also as distinctions within a *unity*. More importantly, in bourgeois commodity production, this unity is not merely the result of analysis by thought. The mediator – the 'fluidity' which sustains the 'unity in difference' – is not the 'fluidity of the concept', but precisely the adaptability of *productive activity* (a material reality, not its concept) which expresses itself now as tailoring and now as weaving, whether considered as the adaptability of an individual's expenditure of his labour-power or as the capacity of the productive system as a whole to move labour from one branch of production to another. The concept 'Fruit' is used by *the thinker* to range over the particular kinds (apples, pears, etc.). It is not the concept 'Fruit' that generates through its own proper activity the apples and pears. However it is not merely the case that 'labour' is a useful concept for *thought* to collect together similar, though differentiated, phenomena: *productive activity itself* is supplied in varying forms according to demand. These forms are not special fixed functions in the way that the species of fruit are biologically determinate. Marx can fairly charge the metaphysician with mistaking his own activity, in moving from apples to pears in thought, as the activity of the concept 'Fruit'. But he himself is not guilty of this, because he reproduces in conceptual form a reality – the *objectively present* unity of the branches of labour in one system of production. More is revealed about this when the matter is examined in the light of historical development. Such a discussion is found in Marx's preliminary work – the so-called *Grundrisse*.

In the 'General Introduction' – written in 1857 – Marx makes some very instructive remarks about the relevance of economic categories. He traces the development of political economy to Adam Smith, who made an immense advance when he rejected all restrictions with regard to the activity that produces wealth – for him it was 'labour as such', not any particular kind. In the following passage Marx links this conceptual advance to its material basis in certain, historically developed, material and social preconditions:

> Now, it might seem that all that had been achieved thereby was to discover the abstract expression for the simplest and most ancient relation in which human beings – in whatever form of society – play the role of producers. This is correct in one respect. Not in another. Indifference[11] towards any specific kind of labour presupposes a very developed totality of real kinds of labour, of which no single one is any longer predominant. As a rule, the most general abstractions arise only in the midst of the richest possible concrete development, where one thing appears as common to many, to all. Then it ceases to be thinkable in a particular form alone. On the other side, this abstraction of labour as such is not merely the mental product of a concrete totality of labours. Indifference towards specific labours corresponds to a form of society in which individuals can with ease transfer from one labour to another, and where the specific kind is a matter of chance for them, hence of indifference. Not only the category, labour, but labour in reality has here become the means of creating wealth in general, and has ceased to be organically linked with particular individuals in any specific form ... The simplest abstraction, then, which modern economics places at the head of its discussions, and which expresses an immeasurably ancient relation

valid in all forms of society, nevertheless achieves practical truth
as an abstraction only as a category of the most modern society.[12]

The simplest way of understanding 'labour' as wealth-
creating activity is to identify the concept with an ahistorical
abstraction. Marx would not, of course, deny the correctness
of this: the bare abstraction 'labour' has perfectly proper
uses – as in the sentence: 'Society can only live by labour,
but, nevertheless, in some societies there are some people
who do not work and hence live off other people's labour'.
Here the concept 'labour' is an ordinary abstract universal
subsuming under itself, generically, the range of labours.
However, Marx goes on to point out that, as a rule, 'the most
general abstractions arise only in the midst of the richest
possible concrete development'. This might be simply a
point about men's epistemological constitution: but it is of
larger significance in a certain form of society. The category
*is not merely the mental product of a concrete totality of
labours*, if the mobility of labour ensures a contingent relation
between the individual and any particular labour he engages
in. In such a situation this apparently ahistorical abstraction
achieves practical truth as an abstraction.

The abstract category 'labour' is, therefore, not merely an
'abstract expression' developed by thought to comprehend
concrete richness. In *this* society, in which 'individuals easily
pass from one type of labour to another', *labour as such* is the
means of creating wealth, not only categorially but 'in
reality'. It is important to know that it is concretely
differentiated; but it is not important for political economy
to further specify it, precisely because of the practical equivalence of labours in capitalist society.

Thus, when individuals are not organically linked with
labour in any specific form, but change their activity as
circumstances demand, the totality of labours carried on in
society, *social labour* in short, is *concretely universal* – self-
differentiating, mobile, and dynamic in a very material sense.

In this section, the category 'labour' has been considered
in relation to the expenditure of social labour as a productive
force (as the primary mediation of production), but the
implicit potential of social labour to realize itself in various

specific activities depends for its expression on the nature of *the relations of production* that organize and develop the productive forces. It is necessary to examine at that (second-order) level of mediation 'the specific manner in which the social character of labour is established'.[13] In particular there is a need to examine the question of the *value of commodities*. It will be seen that the contrast established so far – which refers abstraction to thought processes and concrete universality to material reality – is too simple. It will be shown that a material process of abstraction occurs in value relations, which appears to give 'practical truth' even to 'labour' as an abstraction.

Marx's Approach to Commodity Relations

Marx's labour theory of value must be understood in the context we have just outlined; that is, his view of social labour organized concretely in determinate qualitative forms and quantitative allocations, but capable of indefinite transformations. The problematic that structures his enquiry into commodity-capitalist society may be formulated in terms of the mode of articulation of this underlying reality in and through the *commodity form* of the *product* of labour. He investigates the social *relations of production* expressed in commodity exchange. (Marx is limiting his analysis of economic forms initially to the law governing the allocation of productive labour in society, through the exchange of *products*; he is *not* interested in exchangeable goods *other* than products.) This context of the labour theory of value is not formulated explicitly enough in the exposition of *Capital*, and this has given rise to endless confusion and hostile comment. However, replying to criticism, Marx does spell it out in a letter to his friend Kugelmann:

> Every child knows that a nation which ceased to work, I will not say for a year, but even for a few weeks, would perish. Every child knows too, that the masses of products corresponding to the different needs require different and quantitatively determined masses of the total labour of society. That this *necessity* of the *distribution* of social labour in definite proportions cannot possibly be done away with by a *particular form* of social production but can only change the *mode* of its *appearance* is self-evident. No natural laws can be done away with.

What can change in historically different circumstances is only the *form* in which these laws assert themselves. And the form in which this proportional distribution of labour asserts itself, in a state of society where the interconnection of social labour is manifested in the private exchange of the individual products of labour, is precisely the exchange-value of these products.[14]

This remark, as well as the later sections of the first chapter of *Capital*, including that on commodity fetishism, shows that Marx decisively surpasses the standpoint of classical political economy. That standpoint is well enough exemplified in Moore's above-quoted characterization of Marx's argument, where the problem is stated to be one of 'searching for a common property in terms of which quantities of different commodities can be equated for exchange'. The argument whereby labour is selected as this supposedly necessary common property has been the subject of continual attack from the time of Böhm-Bawerk.[15] Marx's exposition, which looks superficially the same as Ricardo's, provides, in reality, an answer to a different question. The classics attempted to find a common denominator in terms of which all values can be made commensurable and the fractional distribution of the total value between classes examined. Marx's analysis appears to *arrive* at such a common property but, in reality, depends on the presumption that social labour is an aggregate, concretely universal in the sense outlined above, which must be distributed in definite proportions. The law governing this distribution must somehow express itself in the process of commodity exchange since the market in bourgeois society is clearly the relevant proximate determinant of productive activity. Marx advances his law of value as a hypothesis designed to show how labour is allocated qualitatively, and expended with economy, over the branches of the division of labour, in commodity-producing society.

Labour in Commodity Exchange

According to Marx's theory of value, the exchange-values a commodity has against various other commodities are derived from a single value-creating source – labour. The *law of value* holds that the magnitude of value of any product is determined by 'the labour-time socially necessary for its production';[16] from the values of two commodities, determined thus, the requisite exchange-value of one in terms of the other may easily be derived. Marx emphasizes that, 'when commodities are exchanged, their exchange-value manifests itself as something totally independent of their use-value'[17] (although, of course, a commodity must have a use-value if it is to feature in exchange at all). Hence, the distinction between use-value and value in exchange gives rise to a similar opposition in labour itself. For, if products differ in their useful properties, so must the concrete useful labours that shape them. Accordingly, Marx stresses the point that the labour embodied in commodities, as the 'social substance' that relates them together as values, must be viewed as 'human labour in the abstract'.[18]

However its form may vary, concrete useful labour is a necessary condition, independent of the form of society, for the existence of the human race,[19] but in commodity production, Marx holds, labour is not only useful labour but also *value-creating* labour. For Marx this abstract labour is a *determinate social form* of labour that obtains only in relations of commodity production.[20]

The nature of these social relations of commodity-production can be specified. Wherever a division of labour exists labour may be considered *social labour*. However, in a market economy labour is *not directly social* labour. It is directly *private* autonomous labour, even though the product is not destined for consumption by the producer himself, or even for consumption within the local community, but destined for exchange on the market. The labourers enter into economic relations, and thus meet social needs, only in so far as their products are sold on the market as *commodities*. Indeed their products *are* commodities only because they are products of private labours that are independent of one another.[21] By contrast, the products of a peasant family made for their own consumption are differentiated according to the needs to be satisfied, but, says Marx, they do not confront one another reciprocally as commodities, because the family labours are *immediately social* in character.[22]

In a *socialist* economy labour is directly social labour because it is distributed and regulated through a social *plan* (just as labour-processes *within* capitalist enterprises are planned). In a commodity economy labour is *not directly social labour* because production and circulation are fragmented into numerous discrete enterprises and transactions. Every producer operates, formally, independently of the others. Labour is *private autonomous labour*. Hence it has to *become social indirectly* through some mediation.

Where there is no social organization of production, no allocation of labour through deliberate planning, the producers' only social contact with each other is through the act of exchange:

> Since the producers do not come into social contact with each other until they exchange their products, the specific social character of each producer's labour does not show itself except in the act of exchange. In other words, the labour of the individual asserts itself as a part of the labour of society, only by means of the relation which the act of exchange establishes directly between the products, and indirectly, through them, between the producers ... [23]

The products are related as values; and hence, through the production of these values, private labours are socially mediated—but as *abstract* labours. Abstract labour is an 'emerging result',[24] as Marx puts it, of the development of exchange relations among the private producers.

In the spontaneous growth of the division of labour centred in independent commodity producers owning the product as private property, the activity of exchange becomes regularized by the law of value which socially equalizes labours through their reduction to uniform, homogeneous, simple labour, which is qualitatively the same, and therefore differs only in quantity.

This abstraction from the specific forms of labour is not established by thought (hence having merely ideal status): it is 'an abstraction which is made every day in the social process of production'.[25] Marx says:

> When we bring the products of our labour into relation with each other as values, it is not because we see in these articles the material receptacles of homogeneous human labour. Quite the contrary: whenever, by an exchange, we equate as values our different pro-

ducts, by that very act, we also equate, as human labour, the different kinds of labour expended upon them. We are not aware of this, nevertheless we do it.[26]

It is important to understand that the social material character of this process of abstraction leads us to characterize the status of the labour that is embodied in value in a specific way.

The interesting case to compare it with is that in which labours are socially equalized, but in a *predetermined plan* of socialist production (or, if you like, *within* a capitalist enterprise).

Here labour is treated as a universal concretely particularized in definite quantities according to the provisions of the plan. I would argue that such a universal is distinct from (or rather, transformed in) the abstract labour that forms the substance of value. The *processes* of abstraction are so different that we are entitled to refer to the results as very different modes of being of labour.

In a socialist society, labour is *directly* social, and *then* is treated as equal (insofar as a standard man-hour unit is employed) in order to organize the productive system in a rational, efficient manner. In commodity economies labour is directly *private* and only *becomes social* through the mechanisms which equalize it. We find that, in exchange, individual labour 'becomes social labour by assuming the form of its direct opposite, of abstract universal labour'.[27]

What is specific about the exchange relation is that it is precisely in their relation as abstract human labours that the labours crystallized in value become socially recognized: 'in each social form of labour, the labours of different individuals are related to one another as human labours too, but in this case this *relating itself* counts as the *specifically social form* of the labours.'[28]

In a socialist plan the universality of labour is immediately identical with the sociality of labour; the activity of planning presupposes as given the unity-in-difference of the various shapes taken on by concretely universal labour. Each branch of production is qualitatively organized for use and quantitatively organized to produce the assigned number of units with economy of labour-time. In a commodity system the activity of market exchange apportions social labour, qualitatively and quantitatively, through a different second-order mediation, namely, the law of value. In immediately social forms of production, individual labours are mere fractions of the total labour to be allocated. In commodity exchange these individual labours are not mere fractions at the start; they become fractions of the total labour of society only insofar as their universal character achieves practical truth in the value relations of the products entering into commodity exchange. As crystallized in value the fractions of social labour become related to each other in a totality only by a definite rupture with their concrete useful character so that their social character may be imposed on them through their identity as value-creating labours. In the plan the labours do not have to relate to each other as abstract, because they descend from the same source (concretely universal social labour); in commodity production they do not descend from the same source immediately (although, of course, it is still possible to see behind the phenomenal form of private labour the essential unity of labour as the primary mediation between man and nature) because in the private property system of second-order mediations they appear immediately as autonomous private labours. They become universal labours of society only through equating themselves to each other through the exchange of products as values. This exchange not only *materially* (not just formally) abstracts from use, but implicitly equates as homogeneous identical labour the value-creating activities of the labourers. Such labours become socially connected only through the series of equations which arise from this social-material process of abstraction. The abstraction of the planner is conscious and reflects immediately the unity-in-difference of social labour. The abstraction inherent in value-equivalence can occur only through a social process of unconscious character, which equates transitively all the labours carried on in the different branches of production as if each in itself were nothing more than a fraction of a homogeneous substance. In the plan universality exists as a pre-given totality to be apportioned. In commodity production universality emerges as a result – and as an abstract totality – insofar as each producer succeeds in finding a way to express the universal side of his labour, which is effected in value in the form of equivalence of the labours embodied in the commodities exchanging.

Labour as Abstractly Universal

Above it was postulated that social labour could be considered a dynamic, self-differentiated, concretely universal, productive force, appearing as an array of specific labours matching specific social needs. However, it was then pointed out that the relations of production in commodity-producing society are such that labour is not immediately social even though it is determined socially. The objective unity of the branches of labour cannot establish itself as a concrete *whole* regulated by a central plan: rather, the private labours become social only as *abstract*, when they are equated through the exchange of products as commodities. *This* universal form of existence of labour does not express the concrete complementarity of the branches of production. It negates the differences maintained in the division of labour; without negating the negation through expressing their essential unity while recognizing their necessary variety. Being abstract, the labours do not form a structured and differentiated whole, but attain a merely abstract unity.[29] Crystallized in *value*, abstract labour stands separated from, and opposed to, the richness of the concrete. It transcends, but does not preserve, the concrete labours' specificity. 'The various working individuals', says Marx, 'seem to be mere organs of this labour'.[30]

What presents itself to us here is an *abstract universal*. It is abstract because, in value, all labours are credited with the same abstract essence and differ only as quantities of simple average labour. This is not a secondary feature of a mode of accounting – as in socialism – but a fundamental *mode of being* of labour as it appears crystallized in value. This abstractly universal labour can be dynamically expressive only as *more of the same*, insofar as various labour inputs, when valorized, accumulate as capital – a homogeneous whole.

If Stanley Moore's interpretation of Marx's doctrine is recalled, it will be remembered that he writes: 'Why . . . does this substance manifest itself . . . in . . . diversity? Because abstract labour is not static, undifferentiated, dead – but dynamic, self-differentiated, alive. The values of different commodities are externalizations of one labour process, the productive activity of society as a whole'.

This summary is in error. Abstract labour *is* 'static, undifferentiated, dead'. What is 'dynamic, self-differentiated, alive' is the basic productive force, labour-power, expended in all its various forms, and flowing from branch to branch of industry as required. The real question that should be asked is not 'Why diversity?' but 'Why sameness?'. The dynamism of the productive process creates a rich variety of branches of industry, producing a wealth of use-values. Why then do these heterogeneous use-values appear in exchange simply as 'values' – mere quantities of the same thing manifested in the exchange ratios regularly established between commodities? Why does the wealth of bourgeois society appear not in the richness of its real life, but merely as a quantitative amount of convertible currency? In short, why is the primary object of production not the development and satisfaction of a wealth of real needs, but the creation of value?

All this is inherent in the commodity form itself. In the commodity form, the products of labours are related to each other as values. The substance of value is abstract labour 'i.e. labour in which the individual characteristics of the workers are eliminated'.[31] So, as bearers of an abstract essence, the individual value-creating labours achieve a unity in sameness, so to speak, not a unity in difference. The individual's labour is of significance only as an instantiation of its abstract essence, not as a specific contribution to an internally differentiated unity.

Abstract Labour and the Value-Form

I have distinguished between the concrete richness of the useful forms of labour and the negation of these qualitative differences in value, where the labours are unified only as abstractions of themselves, as quantities of an identical homogeneous substance. It has been argued that this is a necessary consequence of the exchange relationship between autonomous producers. The *producers themselves*, however, do not, and do not have to, carry this abstraction in their heads, either as the ground of a theoretical measure or as the ground of a normative principle. The transformation of the various concrete labours into homogeneous abstract labour occurs as a social process, as opposed to a process occurring in individual heads. The problem that arises immediately is to show how an abstraction that is never thought has practical truth and mediates production relations. Marx takes up the point that in treating linen, for example, as a value, as the product of abstract labour, 'one has to abstract from all that which makes it really a thing'. The objective existence of abstract human labour might then be thought 'necessarily an abstract objectivity – a thing of thought'.[32] After all, it is clear that the *natural form* of a commodity, for example 20 yards of linen, embodies only objectified *useful* labour, for example weaving, but not, as such, *abstract* labour. However a commodity can present its value in terms of another commodity (that is as a certain exchange-value), and when it does reflect its value in another commodity, the other commodity plays 'a new role' – a role it acquires *only* when posited as a *value-equivalent*.[33]

Consider the example: '20 yards of linen are worth one coat'. Marx says of the linen: 'By the linen's equating the coat to itself as value, while at the same time *distinguishing* itself from the coat as *object of use* – what happens is that the coat becomes the form of appearance of linen-value as opposed to *linen-body* – its *value-form* is distinguished from its *natural form*.'[34] Thus the linen 'relates itself to the material of the coat as to an immediate materialization of abstract human labour, and thus to labour which is of the same kind as that which is objectified within the linen itself'.[35]

Of course, the coat, as a natural object, is the product of a particular useful labour, tailoring. But this is as it has to be: there are not two different labours lurking in the commodity. Rather: 'the *same* labour is specified in differing and even contradictory ways – in accordance with whether it is related to the *use-value* of the commodity as labour's *product* or related to the *commodity-value* as its merely objective expression.'[36]

Marx illustrates the role of the value-equivalent by pointing out that when we weigh a sugar-loaf with iron weights 'the substance iron, as a measure of weight, represents in relation to the sugar-loaf weight alone'. So 'in our expression of value, the material object, coat, in relation to the linen represents value alone'.[37] Just as heavy objects can be said to have the *same* weight, and *function as weights* independently of their other properties, so commodities share the *same value* and *function* in expressions of value merely *as value* without reference to their various other properties.

However, Marx also points to a disanalogy here. Weight is a natural property of iron but the value-equivalent represents a 'non-natural' property of both commodities, something 'purely social'.[38]

Even when not used in a balance, iron has weight and is involved in various natural relations with other bodies (for example the earth) as a consequence. The balance merely provides a *measure* of weight based on the standard gram or whatever.

However a product in its 'natural form' does not have value. *Only* in exchange is this form of existence *imposed* on it in virtue of its mediating function in the distribution and regulation of labour which is immediately private and is socially equalized as abstract. That a commodity is a value is a *social* fact.[39] Abstract labour provides not merely a measure (socially necessary labour-time) but also the *social substance* of value. In the weight case it is *individually* embodied mass which is represented. In *our* case, commodities are bearers of *social* relations: the value of each has nothing to do with its *individual* production but is measured by the *socially* necessary labour time for the production of *that kind* of commodity.

In Marx's conception, then, abstract labour is a determination evolved in the dialectic of the exchange relationship, commodities being specified as products of abstract labour only insofar as the value-form provides, through the equivalence relationship, the possibility of each commodity externalizing its value in the other such that the labour embodied in the equivalent functions merely as labour in the abstract, independently of its concrete useful character.

Inversion of Abstract and Concrete
It has been argued that, if social labours are *concretely*

universal so far as they create a wealth of *use-values*, they are integrated in the exchange relations of commodity production only as *abstractions* of themselves in the homogeneous totality of *value* produced. We have seen that in a value-equivalent labour counts merely as abstract, qualitatively identical with any other labour, and furthermore, the actual amount of labour embodied is irrelevant because, insofar as we are concerned with values determined through the law of value in terms of *socially necessary* labour-time, the quantity imputed is an aliquot part of the total labour expended by society.

The further point which must now be brought out is *the peculiar relation* between the particular and the universal inherent in value relationships. Here is an exceedingly interesting passage from the first edition of *Capital*:

> Within the value-relation and the value-expression included in it, the abstractly universal does not count as a property of what is concrete, and sensibly-real, but the opposite holds: what is sensibly-concrete counts as mere appearance-form or determinate realization-form of the abstractly universal. It is not that *the labour of tailoring*, which resides for example in the equivalent coat, possesses within the value-expression of linen the *universal property* of also being human labour. The opposite holds: *Being human labour* counts as its *essence*, being the labour of tailoring counts only as the *form of appearance* or *definite form of realization of this its essence* ... This *inversion* whereby the sensibly-concrete counts only as appearance-form of the abstractly universal, and it is not to the contrary that the abstractly universal counts as property of the concrete – this inversion characterizes the value-expression. At the same time it renders difficult its comprehension. If I say: Roman Law and German Law are both law, that is obvious. But if I say, on the other hand, *the* Law, (this abstract entity) *realizes itself* in Roman Law and German Law, (these concrete laws), then the connection becomes mystical.[40]

As the reference to the concept of law shows, Marx is under no illusion about the 'absurd',[41] not to say 'mystical' character of the connection that he is postulating obtains between the abstract-universal and the concrete, within the value relation. Yet, what he would clearly denounce in a theory of law he accepts in his theory of value. Clearly this is because, if he is right, the fetishization of the abstract concept of law is a product of the thinker's mysticism, while the 'mystical character of commodities' arises from the commodity form itself,[42] not from the infection of Marx's mind with Hegel's *Logic*.

Let us examine another relevant passage. If the value of all commodities except one is expressed in terms of this other that is excluded, then a universal equivalent is obtained: 'It is as if alongside and external to lions, tigers, rabbits and all other actual animals, which form grouped together the various kinds, species, sub-species, families etc. of the animal kingdom, there existed also in addition *the animal*, the individual incarnation of the entire animal kingdom'[43], says Marx. This analogy is meant to illuminate the role of the universal equivalent, and the labour it contains: 'The specific labour materialized in it now thereby counts as *universal form of realization* of human labour, as *universal labour*'.[44] Notice here that Marx's discussion of the 'animal' analogy bears a close similarity to the 'fruit' example that he used to ridicule Hegelianism. He by no means now accepts a position he there rejected, because the 'animal' analogy is qualified by the words – 'It is as if ... '. In other words, his thesis that value represents a social substance manifested in the different exchange-ratios cannot depend on a *general* argument covering such cases as fruits and animals. Furthermore the 'animal' analogy is meant to illustrate the strangeness of the situation under discussion in the case of the universal value-body. *It is as if* 'the animal' existed as well as dogs and cats. *It is as if* 'fruit' existed over and above apples and pears. Or, it might be said, *it is as if* human beings could relate to each other, and achieve social intercourse, only through equating themselves to each other as embodying an abstract human essence, instead of directly through mutual needs and interests. But, whereas in the 'fruit' example Marx was caricaturing a metaphysical theory, in the 'animal' case he is illustrating the absurdity of a real social relation.

As values commodities are equatable with one another: so much so that a universal equivalent may be substituted for them all – the money-commodity. In the reproduction of animals a bull cannot stand in for a goat just because some metaphysician declares that it contains the essence of 'the animal'. But, in the reproduction and accumulation of *values* it *is* immaterial what natural form the value-body has. One may put one's wealth into gold, silver, cattle, or even works of art. Furthermore – in order to generate new wealth – one need not enter the sordid sphere of nature at all. In the phenomenon of interest it is as if 'the animal' multiplied through ideal, immaculate, intercourse with itself. (Marx draws attention to the fact that Aristotle understandably considered making 'money of money' the trade 'most contrary to Nature'.)[45]

In sum, value, as the common social substance of commodities, achieves independent existence and acts as a mediator in their circulation.

What all these passages show is that Marx is well aware that his procedure, in postulating an abstract universal as an explanatory concept, bears some comparison with the idealist procedure of exhibiting the 'sensuous-concrete' as the realization of the universal. However, the difference is that he exhibits this relation as the consequence of certain material relations of production – not of the dialectic of 'the concept'. Marx is not to blame for inverting the relation between the concrete and the abstract universal in this case – commodity production is!

The Concrete Universal
In conclusion, I will summarize the philosophical differences between Hegel and Marx on the 'concrete universal'.

In Hegel's philosophy the Notion, or Concept, as the principle which determines both thought and being, is self-related and self-differentiating. It has three phases. The first, or immediate, aspect of the Concept is its *abstract universality*. Its mediation in a variety of finite phenomena gives us the second aspect, *particularity*. These differentiated particulars may at first, in their immediacy, seem foreign to the one meaning of the Concept. However, the fully developed Concept 'comes to itself' finally as, with *concrete universality*, it recognizes these particulars as within itself, and as even in their immediacy still its own meaning. The various forms of existence of the Concept are thus within the concrete universal formed by the whole life of the true Concept.

The materialist criticism of this account draws attention

to the fact that this concept is only *pseudo-concrete* because the relations between the moments are essentially logical – hence the unity-in-difference cannot be sustained onto-logically unless the assumption is made that the world is spiritual. This assumption means that in Hegel the sensuously-concrete particulars are taken up only as abstractions of themselves, and their real material generation, and being, drops out of the picture. Hence the appearance that a conjuring trick is performed when the concept is given flesh.

Marx's concrete universal is not a pan-logical metaphysic, but a determinate mode of being of things only where there is a material basis for it. It has been argued that social labour may be considered concretely universal when the unity-in-difference of individual labours is sustained by the practical truth of the universality of labour as a productive force divisible, according to social need, qualitatively and quantitatively. The relations of the moments are not logical but material. The abstract equivalence of the labours as mere work, and their differentiated forms, may be counterposed in thought but are practically unified, at least where relations of production are immediately social.

While Marx accuses Hegel of inverting the real relationship of the abstract and the concrete in that Hegel gives his logical pattern the status (in speculative truth) of the actual ground of particulars, thus making of the latter the mere hypostasis of the abstract essence, Marx himself describes the relation between concrete labours and their abstract identity (as substance of value) in precisely this way.

However, since the *mode* of abstraction is *material*, arising out of the actual relationships of private producers, Marx is not to blame for thinking it. He far from accepts this inversion as the ultimate truth, as his critical concept of 'commodity fetishism' shows. He shows that *the commodity form of the product of labour* gives rise to the diremption between concrete labours and their abstract essence, and expresses the essential unity of social labour as an *abstract totality*. Unlike Hegel, Marx does not pass off the abstract universal as a concrete whole. His theory is immanently critical of the estrangement of the abstract from the concrete in commodity production. He seeks the supersession of the contradiction not in a speculative reconciliation but in an historical change, through which property is socialized in order to match the increasing socialization of the productive forces.

The immediate organic unity of the local feudal community, and the particularism of the guilds, are dissolved in the universal intercourse established by capitalist-commodity production. No one form of labour, such as agriculture, now predominates over the rest – wealth is created by a wide variety of labours. However, the unity of social labours is mediated only in that each and every value-creating productive activity counts merely as an abstraction of itself.

Social labour can come to itself as a synthesis of these moments, as concretely universal, insofar as a change in the relations of production overcomes the estrangement between them. Socialism is the genuine unity of the many in the one.

A Note on Secondary Literature

In spite of the fact that Marx openly admitted his debt to Hegel, and spoke of 'what is rational' in Hegel's dialectic, curiously little attention has been paid to this hint by the commentators. Lenin himself remarked on the necessity of studying *Capital* in the light of Hegel's *Logic*, and deduced gleefully from the evident failure of Marxists to do so that they had never understood Marx.[46] Nonetheless there are still those today, Louis Althusser for example, who hold the view that Marx merely flirts with Hegelian expressions because he did not yet have 'an adequate concept with which to think what he produced'.[47]

It was shown above that problems associated with Marx's concept of 'abstract labour' are central to the comprehension of the first chapter of *Capital* and lead us into complex dialectical relations. Yet the most important writers on Marx's value theory tend to assure us that there is no real problem here.

Ernest Mandel says:

> But if these commodities are each the products of a specific kind of labour, they are also the products of *social human labour*, that is, of a

part of the total labour time available to a particular society, and on the economy of which society is based . . . . This is the fact that makes commodities commensurable; it is this general human labour – called abstract labour because abstraction is made from its specific nature, just as when one adds together three apples, four pears and five bananas one has to abstract from their specific qualities so as to be left with merely twelve *fruits* – that is the basis of exchange value.[48]

It is rather entertaining in view of the discussion above that Mandel uses the example of 'fruit' in order to illustrate the evolution of an abstraction. The discussion has shown that this is inappropriate in that the fixity of the species of fruit does not illustrate the mobility of labour; while if one is thinking of abstract labour as the substance of value, mediating the intercourse of commodity producers, the analogy fails to show the possibility of the material production of the abstraction, not to speak of the inversion of abstract and concrete that obtains when a commodity counts just as a value and the labour embodied in it counts merely as a hypostasis of the abstractly universal.

Mandel adds in a note to the above passage that 'the idea of "abstract labour" could not arise until the appearance of the *mobility of labour-power* in the capitalist era', when jobs become interchangeable. It is curious that Mandel refers here merely to the arrival of the *idea* – I would argue that only this material reality gives the idea *practical truth* and provides a valid foundation for the law of value.

Paul Sweezy gives the matter the same emphasis. He claims that Marx's concept of 'abstract labour' is 'quite straightforward' and by no means 'slightly mysterious' for it merely refers to 'what is common to all productive activity'; and then he adds that 'The very nature of capitalist production . . . promotes a degree of labour mobility never before approached . . . '[49]

Again the question is not treated with sufficient precision here. Abstract labour must be specified as the *social form* of labour in commodity production, and, as we have seen above, contrary to Sweezy, there is something 'slightly mysterious' about it.

The Soviet scholar I. I. Rubin was the author of a

masterly exposition of the problematics of the first chapter of *Capital*: the recently rediscovered *Essays on Marx's Theory of Value*. Although he rarely mentions Hegel, this did not save him from being liquidated in the name of a battle against 'Menshevik idealists, who treated Marx's revolutionary method in the spirit of Hegelianism.'[50]

The value of his exposition is that it shows how Marx's categories are rooted in the social relations of production. Thus, with regard to the problem of the twofold character of labour in commodity producing society, he says: 'Concrete labour is the definition of labour in terms of its *material-technical properties*. Abstract labour includes the definition of *social forms* of organization of human labour. This is not a generic and specific definition of labour, but the analysis of labour from two standpoints: the material-technical and the social.'[51]

He insists on the distinction of the social organization of labour in a commodity-capitalist society from that of any other form of socially-equalized labour such as that established in a socialist plan of production. If any complaint may be levelled against Rubin's presentation it is that, in his anxiety to exhibit the meaning of Marx's work in terms of the social relations underlying value, he neglects the full complexity of the value mediations themselves; in particular, he provides no proper account of the forms of value and the hypostatization involved there.

M. Itoh considers that at the beginning of *Capital* Marx follows the Ricardian approach in that he abstractly counterposes value and use-value and hence is led to see abstract labour as a determination pertaining only to the creation of value, failing to mention it in the later discussion (Chapter 7, Section 1) on the labour process as a process of production of use-values by concrete labours. For Itoh 'concrete labour is always nothing but the concrete forms of abstract human labour'; he also complains that 'Rubin's "socially equalized labour" must have an abstract character and count only quantitatively, in contrast with concrete labour'.[52]

Rubin can be supported on the ground that value is an historically specific form of the labour product (as Itoh admits), and therefore the nature of the labour constituting

the social substance of value must have an historically specific
form expressing the social character of labour in an organization of production in which the product must take on a
commodity form: it (abstract labour) cannot be the mere
genus. It is true that labour equalized in a socialist plan of
production is also thereby bound up with a process of
abstraction, or, as I would prefer to say, it forms part
of the universal labour of society and it is consciously organized as such by the planning process. However, I tried
above to demonstrate the mediated process of abstraction
peculiar to the equalization of labours through the values of
their products, as opposed to the equalization of immediately
social labours.

Finally, let us consider the position of Lucio Colletti who
considers the relation of Marx to Hegel's dialectic. For
Colletti abstract labour is the product of a material abstraction
and for this reason he equates it with *alienated* labour: 'it is an
activity which does not represent an *appropriation* of the
objective, natural world so much as an *expropriation* of
human subjectivity, a separation of labour "capacity" or
"power" conceived as the totality of physical and intellectual
attitudes, from man himself.'[53] Colletti sees parallels between
Marx's critique of Hegel's mystifying logic, his early critique
of the state which makes an abstract whole of society, and his
analysis of the value relationships of commodities: the
argument always 'hinges upon the hypostatizing, the reifying,
of abstractions and the consequent inversion of subject and
predicate'.[54]

However, Colletti finds it difficult to unite his eager
endorsement of Marx's exposure of the Hegelian speculative
inversion, with his appreciation of the theory of alienation
as one involving the theory of contradiction. He argues that
Marx's discovery of contradictions in capitalism does not
lead to an inverted Hegelianism:

> For Marx, capitalism is contradictory not because it is a *reality* and
> all realities are contradictory, but because it is an *upside-down*,
> inverted reality (alienation, fetishism) ... All the same, if it is true
> that this does not rehabilitate *Diamat*, it is nonetheless true that it
> confirms the existence of two aspects in Marx: that of the scientist
> and that of the philosopher.[55]

Colletti seems to tend to the view that any analogue of Hegelian patterns in reality must lead a materialist to criticize it. However, it has been shown above that there is a material analogue of the 'concrete universal' which is acceptable (when we analysed labour-power or social labour in terms of it). It is indeed the attempt to recuperate the concrete universal which distinguishes my position from Colletti's. Colletti demonstrates better than anyone else the idealist hypostatization of the abstract essence in the concrete particulars manifested in Hegel's philosophy, the abstract citizen, and the value-forms: but what should one conclude from this? One tends to be directed to the view that concrete particulars are ontologically fundamental, and that universality is essentially abstract. I disagree. Marx counterposes to the abstract citizen, not the bourgeois individual (who 'may in his ... imagination ... inflate himself into an atom'[56]) but the social individual! He envisages labour, freed from its subordination to an abstract whole, as the form of realization of this social individual, a universal mediation of the species such that 'our products would be so many mirrors in which we saw reflected our essential nature'.[57] If Hegel takes the movement of thought as the autonomous demiurge of actual human agents, we should not counterpose the thinking individual to this, for the 'intellectual wealth of the individual depends entirely on the wealth of his real connections'.[58] When Feuerbach rejected the Hegelian inversion of subject and predicate he retreated, according to Marx, to a view of the human essence as an internal dumb generality,[59] whereas Marx opened the road to the social totality mediated by practical activity. The universal character of this activity, and its estrangement in value relationships, constitute his problematic.

Notes

The above paper is a later version of an argument advanced by me in a paper in *Inquiry* (1978) that replies more directly to S. Moore (*Inquiry*, 1971), and to T. Carver (*Inquiry*, 1975) and U. Steinvorth (*Inquiry*, 1976). I would like to thank Rachel Kahn-Hut (San Francisco), Ian Steedman (Manchester), David Ruben (Essex), Wal Suchting (Sydney), Kate Soper (Sussex), and John Mepham for critical comments on various drafts.

1 Marx remarks that in the chapter on value especially, he 'coquetted with the modes of expression' peculiar to Hegel. *Capital*, I, 'Afterword,' (Moscow 1961), p. 20.

2 *Ibid.* It is worth remarking that there are two versions of the first chapter. For the second edition Marx rewrote it in more didactic fashion. (Marx reports on the changes in the 'Afterword', *Capital*, I, p. 12). In the process of reworking he drops two direct references to Hegel's *Logic* and is less coquettish with Hegelian terminology, Nonetheless the *substance* of the matter is unaffected. Marx admits (*Capital*, I, p. 8) that 'the section on value-form' is a difficult one, and, in fact, this section is completely reworked for the second edition. The earlier, rather more Hegelian, version of it brings out better the aspects that I wish to emphasize, and I shall sometimes cite that below.

3 *Capital*, I, p. 19.

4 Marx and Engels *Collected Works*, vol IV (London 1975), pp. 57–9. J. N. Findlay defends Hegel on this point: 'There is no trace in his practice, despite the use of some generative metaphors, of any attempt to beget what is Specific or Individual out of the mere Universality of The Notion'. *Hegel: A Re-Examination* (London 1958), p. 226.

5 *Op. cit.* p. 60, see Marx, *The Poverty of Philosophy*, ch. 2, 1, first observation, *Collected Works*, VI (London 1976), pp. 162–5).

6 *Capital*, I, p. 19.

7 Stanley Moore, 'Marx and the origins of Dialectical Materialism', *Inquiry*, XIV (1971), p. 424.

8 *Capital*, I, p. 41, see also Marx to Engels 24 August 1967, *Selected Correspondence* (Moscow 1965), p. 192.

9 Karl Marx *A Contribution to the Critique of Political Economy* (London 1971), p. 20.

10 *Capital*, I, p. 43–4.

11 In his edition of the 'Introduction' Carver has the following note: '"indifference" (Gleichgültigkeit). The term has a philosophical sense, which might apply here, as "want of difference in nature or character; substantial equality or equivalence" (OED *sv* Indifference 5). It also

figures in Hegel's *Logic*: "Being is the abstract equivalence [Gleichgültigkeit] for which ... the expression indifference [Indifferenz] has been employed" [Hegel (1812), 375]. Thus this passage might be read as "The abstract equivalence of determinate forms of labour presupposes..."' *Karl Marx : Texts on Method* (Oxford 1975), p. 77, n. 39.

The suggestion is, therefore, that 'indifference' has very little to do with an attitude originating in the labourer's own insensitivity (to real distinction), or apathy (to anything that might happen to him). The emphasis is not on psychological insensitivity, but on the practical equivalence of labours which makes the simple abstraction 'labour' the valid and relevant concept without further specification.

12 *Grundrisse*, M. Nicolaus (tr.) (Harmondsworth 1973), pp. 104–105.

13 Marx, *Contribution*, p. 32; see Marx's 'Notes on Adolph Wagner' (in *Texts on Method*), p. 207.

14 11 July 1968. Marx and Engels, *Selected Correspondence*, p. 209.

15 E. Böhm-Bawerk, *Karl Marx and the Close of his System* (London 1975), ch. 4.

16 *Capital*, I, p. 39.

17 *Ibid*. p. 38.

18 *Ibid*.

19 *Ibid*. pp. 42–3.

20 As early as 1847 Marx says that 'economic categories are only the theoretical expressions, the abstractions, of the social relations of production'. (*The Poverty of Philosophy*, ch. 2, 1, second observation, *Collected Works*, VI, p. 165). Classical political economy, taking the existing mode of production for granted, never asked the question 'why labour is represented by the value of its product and labour-time by the magnitude of that value' (*Capital*, I, p. 80). Marx is interested in the 'social form in which the labour-product is presented in contemporary society' – which is *not* indicated by the useful properties possessed on the basis of its *natural* form. (*Contribution*, pp. 27–8).

21 *Capital*, I, p. 42.

22 *Ibid*. p. 78.

23 *Ibid*. p. 73.

24 *Contribution*, p. 45.

25 *Ibid*. p. 30. 'Can there be abstraction other than by thought? No modern thinker except Marx has answered this question in the affirmative.' A. Sohn-Rethel, *Radical Philosophy* VI (1973), p. 31.

26 *Capital*, I, p. 74.

27 *Contribution*, p. 34.

28 This quotation is from the first edition of *Capital*, I, ch. 1: *Value: Studies by Marx*, A Dragstedt (tr. and ed.) (London 1976), p. 32.

29 See Lucio Colletti's 'Introduction' to Marx's *Early Writings* (Harmondsworth 1975), which shows the thematic unity between Marx's early critique of the state and his critique of political economy. Colletti does not attempt, however, to recuperate the 'concrete universal',

as I do here, or, more generally, to consider 'what is rational in Hegel' (Marx).

30 *Contribution*, p. 30.

31 *Ibid.* p. 28.

32 *Capital*, I, ch. 1 (1st edn.), in *Value : Studies by Marx*, p. 19.

33 It is here that Marx has recourse to such Hegelian expressions as *Reflexionsbestimmungen* – 'determinations of reflections' or 'reflex-categories', *Capital*, I, p. 57n.

34 *Capital*, I, ch. 1 (1st edn.), in *Value : Studies by Marx*, p. 20.

35 *Ibid.*

36 *Capital*, I, ch. 1 (1st edn.), in *Value : Studies by Marx*, p. 16. (I have substituted 'ways' for 'manner'.) For an interesting commentary on this formulation of the duality of labour see I. I. Rubin *Essays on Marx's Theory of Value* (Detroit 1972), p. 146 n20.

37 *Capital*, I, p. 56–7.

38 *Ibid.* compare *Ibid.*, p. 47, 'The value of commodities is the very opposite of the coarse materiality of their substance, not an atom of matter enters into its composition . . . The value of commodities has a purely social reality . . . It follows as a matter of course that value can only manifest itself in the social relation of commodity to commodity.'

39 For an interpretation of Marx's theory of the commodity based on the notion of 'constitutive rules' see A. Anton, 'Commodities and Exchange', *Philosophy and Phenomenological Research* (March 1974).

40 *Value : Studies by Marx*, pp. 56–7. This passage is from an appendix to the first edition of Volume I of *Capital* designed to provide further clarification of the value-form (= chap. 1 Sec. 3 in the second edition). This 'double exposition' is suppressed, Marx says in the second edition, because the whole of Sec. 3 is reworked.
(Dragstedt's rendition has been corrected in the light of a much superior translation of the appendix by Roth and Suchting—*Capital and Class*, IV, Spring 1978.)

41 *Capital*, I, p. 76.

42 *Ibid.*, p. 71.

43 *Value : Studies by Marx*, p. 27. This passage from *Capital*, chap. 1, appears only in the first edition. Hegel says: 'When the universal is made a mere form and co-ordinated with the particular, as if it were on the same level, it sinks into a particular itself. Even common sense in everyday matters is above the absurdity of setting a universal *beside* the particulars. Would any one, who wished for fruit, reject cherries, pears, and grapes, on the ground that they were cherries, pears, or grapes, and not fruit?' *The Logic of Hegel*, W. Wallace (tr.), being Part One of the *The Encyclopaedia of the Philosophical Sciences*, 3rd edn. (Oxford 1975).
True – yet in the market place vendors will reject various particular values on the ground that they are not *money*, their externalised identity as values.

44 *Ibid.*

45 *Capital*, I, pp. 164–5.
46 *Collected Works*, XXXVIII (Moscow 1961), p. 180.
47 L. Althusser and E. Balibar, *Reading Capital* (London 1970), p. 29.
48 *Marxist Economic Theory*, I (London 1968), p. 65.
49 *The Theory of Capitalist Development* (London 1946), pp. 30–2.
50 Quoted in R. Rosdolsky, *The Making of Marx's 'Capital'* (London 1977), p. 570.
51 *Essays on Marx's Theory of Value*, Miloš Samardžija and Fredy Perlman (trs.) (Detroit 1972), p. 141.
52 'A Study of Marx's Theory of Value' in *Science and Society* (Autumn 1976), pp. 320, 321n.; see also U. Steinvorth in *Inquiry*, XIX (1976).
53 *From Rousseau to Lenin* (London 1972), p. 87.
54 'Introduction' to Karl Marx, *Early Writings* (Harmondsworth 1975), p. 39.
55 "Marxism and the dialetic' in *New Left Review*, 93 (1975), p. 29.
56 Marx and Engels, *The Holy Family* in *Collected Works*, IV, p. 120.
57 'Comments on James Mill' (1844); Marx and Engels, *Collected Works*, III (London 1975), pp. 727–8. *Early Writings* (the Penguin edition) gives the last word as 'natures' (p. 278) thus importing unfortunate individualistic connotations contrary to the spirit of the passage.
58 Marx and Engels, *The German Ideology* in *Collected Works*, V (London 1976), p. 51.
59 'On Feuerbach', Thesis Six, in *Collected Works*, V.

4 *Dialectic and Ontology*

MILTON FISK

Nonsense or Triviality

THE analytical school of philosophy has proven itself very durable. It has undergone a variety of changes of form. The common thread is unmistakeable as analysts turn from Platonist to nominalist stances, from instrumentalist to scientific realist world-views, and from ordinary language to canonical language methodologies. Under each of its many forms, analysis is characterized by an ontology that separates it from the notable alternatives. This ontology is best described as an atomist one in that the basic entities in it are simples. The durability of the analytical school has less to do with the fashionableness of the various forms it has taken than with the fact that the atomist ontology of the school fits in with other broad features of the culture of this society.

The ontological core of the analytical school has been the basis for its attitude toward the dialectical school that originated with Hegel and Marx. The interesting thing about this attitude is that it never includes the worry, 'Is the dialectician, perhaps, coming from a completely different ontological standpoint?' Thus the dialectical school gets dismissed from either of two equally unhelpful directions.

On the one hand, dialectic is held to be nonsense. After all, it denies the basic sense-giving theses of analysis: it asserts the non-existence of distinctions where there is nonetheless complexity and it asserts the reality of contradictions. Complexes that do not incorporate distinctions are incompatible with the central thesis of analysis that clarity comes from pursuing reality to its basis in simples. And contradictions are incompatible with the logic that analysis uses as its tool for making sense out of language and the world.[1]

On the other hand, there is the conciliatory response that claims to incorporate dialectic, without loss, into analysis. This response begins by noting that the two schools speak languages that are at first unintelligible to one another. But it concludes by noting that if analysts would only be a bit patient with dialecticians they could show the dialecticians how to translate their obscurantist prose into model analyese. In fact, once this translation is made, it appears that the dialectical school has said nothing beyond utter triviality anyway. The claim that distinctions get fuzzy within tight complexes translates into something about the need to recognize two-way causal connections between the components of organic and of social systems. There are no purely independent variables, and somehow this gets mystified by dialectic into a denial that there are clear distinctions within organic wholes.[2] The claim that contradictions are real translates into something straightforwardly scientific, such as that for every action there is an equal and opposite reaction.

All of this misses the point entirely. Yet it is not surprising, in view of the paradigmatic character of the ontological core of the analytical school, that many self-proclaimed dialecticians have grasped at the conciliatory response of the analytical school as a golden opportunity to carry truth to the unbelieving.[3] What in fact they have done is to disembowel dialectic.

The point missed is that dialectic is characterized by an ontology comprehensible only in a tradition that analysts and their forebears rejected long ago. Their historical memories do not serve them well enough to remind them of the struggle with that tradition. They have been completely occupied with changes within their own framework. And thus when they are presented with a position, such as dialectic, that stems from that earlier tradition, their response is to treat it as the child of an upstart confusion, rather than of an old heresy. This forgetfulness is promoted by the fittingness of the atomist ontology with the culture. It is still worth pointing out some of the basic features of the ontology of complexes, which had its classical expression in Aristotle, and some of the ways it was varied to provide the basis for the dialectical world-view. Whatever the earlier socio-cultural basis for the rejection of the tradition of the ontology of complexes, there is now a strong basis for revising that rejection and for accepting the world-view of dialectic.

The View in Brief

The dialectical tradition is far from monolithic. There are important differences between Sartre and Gramsci, between Engels and Lenin, between Trotsky and Bukharin, and between Lukacs and Mao. The dialectical world view shared by all of them, if there is one, may well be only an insignificant least common denominator. Thus, rather than trying to find what is common between them, it will be more rewarding to reconstruct what is living in the dialectical tradition from a foundation that takes account of the historical experience accumulated within the tradition.

The foundation to be used here has three sides to it: complexity, contradiction, and essence. Each of these notions is the focus of a thesis characteristic of a reconstructed dialectic of a very general nature. The first thesis has to do with the composition of entities:

> *Thesis of Complexity:* whatever is an entity in its own right is complex.

The entities that result from analysis may well be simple, but it is a mistake to take them as having a being of their own. The second thesis states why contradictions are important to dialectic:

> *Thesis of Contradiction:* internal contradictions are a necessary source of change that are resolved only by change.

Without internal contradictions, entities are characterized by nothing more than their self-sameness, and thus have no potential for change. The third thesis has to do with the source of contradictions:

> *Thesis of Essence:* at least one contradiction is of the essence of every entity that exists in its own right.

If internal contradictions were all accidental, changes resulting from them would not have to be characteristic of the systems with them. And thus contradictions could not be the basis for laws of the development of those systems.

These three theses differ from the three time-honoured laws of dialectic: these were the law of the unity of opposites, the law of the transition from quantitative change to qualitative difference, and finally the law of the negation of the negation.[4] The theses asserted here for a reconstructed general dialectic differ from these three laws in two respects. First, the theses of complexity, contradiction, and essence attempt to point to very general features of entities that are behind some, at least, of the laws of dialectic. Second, these theses try to remain neutral on the issue of how changes occur. It was to this issue that the law of the transition from quantity to quality was addressed.

For example, the thesis of complexity is more general than the law of the unity of opposites.[5] That law says that salient oppositions are not to be treated as external but as having their source in the being in which they reside. Complexity does indeed imply opposition, as we shall see. But it says nothing about the terms of the opposition being derived from a common root. Even the thesis of essence does not say that salient oppositions have such a root, but only that at least one opposition that resides in an entity will have such a root. As far as reconstructed general dialectic is concerned there may be salient oppositions that are either accidental or external or both.

The thesis of contradiction is more general than the law of the transition from quantity to quality. This thesis is neutral on the question as to whether there must be quantitative changes at all for there to be qualitative changes. In a materialist dialectic there will be an emphasis on the quantitative basis, but not here in general dialectic. The change from free-enterprise to monopoly is not, for the materialist, an inner development of the idea of capitalism, as it would be if qualitative change took place without quantitative change. It is, rather, a development which presupposes quantitative changes in the concentration of the labouring population, of industrial production, and of financial resources.

It is important to introduce now the generalized notion of contradiction to be employed here in order to see how change resolves contradiction. According to this notion, the root of contradiction is complexity itself. An entity in its own right is complex in the sense that it is a unity of diverse and hence multiple aspects – properties, dispositions, natures, physical parts. The entity is *contradictory* precisely in that, as an entity in its own right, it is one and yet, as an entity with multiple aspects, it is not one. To resolve such a contradiction requires that the one that is multiple no longer exists, either because it changes into another entity or because some polarity within it disappears even while it continues to exist. The essential contradictions of the thesis of essence, which will be the prime concern here, can be resolved only by the destruction of the initial entity and the emergence of a new one, which will have its own contradictions.

The law of the negation of the negation follows immediately from the thesis of contradiction, on this interpretation of contradiction. The initial negation within any entity will, I shall show, be the break-up of the self-sameness of the entity resulting from the fact that the entity is of a certain kind. The unity of the entity is then pitted against the multiplicity constituted by its unity and its kind. This is no adventitious conjuction of opposite forces, but is is a negation present wherever there are entities.[6] The contradiction between being one and being many results from the negation of bare unity by the kind. This contradiction will be resolved only by change, according to the second thesis. This change is the negation of the initial negation in that it destroys the contradiction generated by the initial negation but not in that it restores the initial bare self-sameness. It restores nothing, but destroys the entity and generates a new one with a similar contradictory structure.

The thesis of essence, as noted above, does not imply the law of the unity of opposites. What the thesis of essence does that none of the laws of dialectic did is to put within dialectic an explicit recognition of the fact that entities are law-governed and that the laws governing them will centre on contradictory features of entities. Moreover, if contradictions were adventitious, they could be resolved by patch-up changes rather than fundamental ones. Also, the thesis of essence when conjoined with the thesis of contradiction yields the result that changes resolving essential contradictions are essential changes. They are the natural self-development of entities.

Dialecticians are fond of criticizing non-dialectical accounts as 'one-sided', 'formalist', and 'abstract'. The thesis of complexity is behind these criticisms. For, behind each of them is the idea that something which is not an entity in its own right and which has been discovered by a process of analysis is being dignified with the status of being an entity in its own right. Thus one side of an entity, the form of an entity, or something abstracted from an entity comes to be treated as though it could be, and also be understood, in isolation from that entity.

The addiction to a formalist ontology is, though, not as deep-seated as is the horror of contradiction among atomist philosophers. Contradiction is driven back by them into subjectivity, as though there were some better account of its possibility there.[7] But the atomist tradition never allowed the notion of contradiction its legitimate generalization. Frege could generalize the notion of mathematical function to allow for concepts to be functions whose values are truth values. But the atomist ontology stood in the way of generalizing the notion of contradiction from the special case of logical contradiction to the general idea of the unity of the diverse.

How is the generalization made? It is made by focusing on the fact that a *de re* logical contradiction involves a multiplicity of terms within a unity. It so happens that in this case of the unity of the diverse one of those terms is the negate of the other. Because the terms have this relation such a multiplicity within a unity is impossible. But in generalizing from the special case of logical contradiction, it is not the special relation of the terms that is the focus of attention but the diversity within unity. And unities involving terms standing in different relations may indeed be possible. The impossibility of a *de re* logical contradiction is due not to the fact that it is a unity of the diverse but that it is a unity of terms one of which is the negation of the other. The contradiction of unity by diversity is common to cases in which the diversity of terms is characterized by different relations. If this unity of what is not one is our focus in looking at contradictions, then the specific character of the relation of the terms in the unity becomes inessential to the contradiction. In this way Hegel was able to give contradiction its legitimate generalization.[8] But it was possible only because he was not tied to the atomist view that there could be no genuine unity of the diverse. This generalization shifts the attack on real contradiction by atomists to the proper point. It was always billed as an attack on eccentrics who either believe in real logical contradictions or else confuse logical contradictions with what are mere external oppositions. But the generalization makes clear that the attack is not really on such strawpersons. The attack is on the ontology of complexes itself. For what is being denied by the atomist is that there can be a genuine unity of the diverse.

The Warrant

Since the basic shift involved in adopting dialectic is the shift to an ontology of complexes, more needs to be said about that ontology. First, something needs to be said about the warrant for such an ontology. And then, something needs to be said, in the following section, about the fundamental multiplicity that characterizes entities.

Ontology as it is known in the modern Western world is never far removed from the process of inquiry. It is both parasitic upon and regulative of inquiry. An ontology can rationalize the existing limits upon the practice of science with a conception of being that has no place for a transcendence of those limits. That conception of being is then internalized in scientific practice through regulating this practice.

Atomist ontology, if it allows for laws at all, assumes that simples of themselves have certain connections among themselves. The ontology of complexes, however, is committed to the view that of themselves simples have no connections to one another. They are connected in determinate ways only relative to the complexes of which they are the parts. This relativity of connections among parts to complexes is not at all the same thing as the variation of a connection through a variation of boundary conditions. For a connection among simples that is relative to boundary conditions is of

the same kind even when the influences making up the
boundary conditions vanish. But here, dependence on a
complex is a condition for there being a connection at all.

Because of its stand on connections, atomism is faced with
both a practical and a theoretical difficulty. The practical
difficulty is that in so far as atomism regulates inquiry there is
a built-in tendency to develop theories so obviously one-sided
that they have little use.

A case in point is the Deweyian theory that significant
social reform can be brought about through education.[9]
Dewey knew there was a hierarchical division of labour in
industry that required for its reproduction the inculcation of
certain attitudes through the educational system. And he also
knew that there was an impulse in numerous persons to
reform the society. His theory of reform through education
required that this reform impulse, when linked to education,
could overturn the demands made on education by the
hierarchical division of labour. He was considering the
reform impulse and the hierarchical division as isolated
phenomena. Quite naturally, then, he saw no reason why the
reform impulse could not outweigh the demands of that
division of labour. Yet both the reform impulse and the
hierarchical division of labour are analytical components of
the overall system of profit. Any connexion between them
must be seen as sustained by that system. And clearly the
connection postulated by Dewey to confirm his theory of
reform through education could not be sustained by that
system since the hierarchical division of labour is a practical
necessity for it.

Social science abounds with like examples of the one-sided
theories that are based on the view that connections can be
postulated between simples where no whole is envisaged to
sustain those connections. What is happening here is that an
atomist ontology that has rationalized the limits of a certain
scientific practice has begun to regulate that practice. The
overall culture limits scientific practice. In particular, the
culture discourages the explanation of the failure of certain
connections to develop between certain aspects of the society
by reference to the overall social arrangement itself. It
discourages such an explanation especially when developing

such connections is called for by the ideals of the society.

The theoretical difficulty is that there is a crisis in the foundations of inquiry due to the atomist ontology and unresolvable by it.

Descartes[10] had set science on a foundation of connections between simples, and Locke[11] had pushed it back to powers, which depended on textures of parts that exhausted substances. Locke's emphasis on powers did not, then, commit him to an ontology of complexes. Behind these powers were arrangements of simples, and these simples – material parts – were for him irreducible reality. There was a wide opening for a sceptical attack here and into it stepped David Hume. One could conceive, Hume noted, any relations whatsoever between simples. How, then, could Descartes pretend to intuit specific connections, and how could Locke pretend that a given texture of simples was the basis for one power rather than another?

The mere raising of the question destroyed the atomist foundations of inquiry, and they have never since been reconstructed. Hume, as a refiner of atomism, was unwilling to accept the possibility that his argument was a *reductio* of the premiss of atomism rather than of the premiss of connections. Only a few who have worked within the analytical tradition have seen that, in order to have an ontology that is compatible with the belief that inquiry can give one some warrant for believing even in regularities, it is necessary to reject the atomist ontology. Among the few was C.D. Broad who saw that the supposition of natural kinds, as defining complexes to which various properties belong, was needed to make induction a reasonable practice.[12]

Where It Starts

It is not enough to posit the contradictory nature of things. That leaves one with a mystery. Why, after all, could they not be non-contradictory? But to get beyond this mystery, one could posit either an external or an internal reason for contradiction. It would surely be a help to know that there is some external reason, such as that change requires contradiction. Yet even that leaves in the dark why nature should oblige one by changing. Maybe things are such that, as the

Parmenideans and Kantians have held, change does not belong to a world of things in themselves but only to their appearances. Things would not then be in themselves contradictory. In the end, the search for an internal reason·for contradiction cannot be avoided.

The mystery is cleared away only by getting back to fundamentals about entities. Each of them is the same as itself. And each of them belongs to some kind. Taken together these claims amount to the truism that every entity is a unit of a certain kind. If this is indeed where contradiction starts, then there is no trouble at all in seeing that contradiction is a pervasive feature of entities. But to show that contradiction starts here depends on being clear that unity and kind belong to an entity of itself and not through its relations to other entities. For, what needs to be shown is that things are by nature contradictory, not that they become contradictory because of the relations they happen to develop to other entities.

If in fact entities were formless units, if that is they were particulars bare of all differentiating features, then entities would not be contradictory.[13] It is precisely the atomist conception of the individual that makes basic individuals formless units. There may well be the assumption that these units are differentiated by their relations to properties. But, for the atomist, these properties are not components that make an individual complex. They are external to the individuals they are called upon to differentiate. Contradictions do indeed lurk in the very conception of entities having properties by being related, tied, or what have you to properties that are not components of them. But these are external contradictions — contradictions not within the make up of a single entity but in the interconnection of entities that are not the same as one another. And the upshot of these external contradictions is that entities conceived as formless units cannot have properties through relationships.

There is then no alternative to treating the kind of an entity as something to which it belongs of itself. Its being of a certain kind is an internal condition, a condition that arises from the entity itself.

Similarly, an entity is the same as itself on an internal

basis.[14] It is not the same as itself because it is at a different space-time location from any other entity. On such a basis, self-sameness is a function of other entities being related to a given entity, not a function of the given entity itself. Nor is an entity the same as itself because of the descriptive properties it has. The self-sameness of indiscernibles makes self-sameness depend on properties, when in fact an entity's being self-same is a condition for its having any property whatsoever.

Atomist philosophy has all along insisted that where there is difference there is distinction. That is, entities that are different must, for the atomist, not be the same entities. But there can be no ontology of complexes without denying this base premiss of atomism. The components – properties, dispositions, natures, parts – of entities that exist in their own right are not themselves entities that exist in their own right. They are attached to the complex of which they are components and are not, then, really distinct from it. The components of an individual are certainly different from that individual. They can be differentiated by the simple fact that the individual has features its components do not have: the individual is, say, soluble in water but solubility, which is one of its components, is not soluble in water. Nonetheless, since the components are not distinct particulars from the individual that has them, they have a status as particulars only as the same as the individual that has them. The solubility of this grain of salt is, then, a something only as the same as the grain. And since the solubility and the shape of the grain are both the same as the grain, they are the same particular as one another, while remaining different. This is grating on a raw nerve for atomists, but it is the core of the ontology beginning with Aristotle and going through Hegel to the materialist dialectic of the Marxists.

As a consequence, the unity and kind of an entity will be different but non-distinct aspects of it. How else could they be internal features – which it was just shown they must be – of a given entity? This difference is in fact contradiction as it was generalized above. For, contradiction was difference in unity, and here we have terms – unity and kind – that in any given case, require unity in regard to sameness, even though they lack unity in regard to difference. As constituting an internal difference, unity and kind make an entity with them contradictory.[15] They cannot be called opposites just because they make the entity with them contradictory. It is the opposition of multiplicity within sameness that is generated by the difference between unity and kind that exists when there is a contradiction.

There is an *instability* about multiplicity within unity that atomists take to be an *impossibility* of multiplicity within unity. The instability comes from the fact that diversification within a whole is not an automatic phenomenon; it requires a pitting of some principle, internal or external, of diversification against the undifferentiated substance of the whole. The tension that keeps the whole diversified must be maintained and this means realizing the potential associated with each and every element in the multiplicity. Change is the response of diversity to the possibility of its withdrawing back into undifferentiated substance.[16] If static forms were able to maintain diversity, this would indicate that the diversity was not actually a diversity within a whole, which as a unit is opposed to the tension the existence of that diversity implies, but was a diversity spread among entities assumed to stand on their own. The assumption by the ontology of complexes that complexes are not just aggregates but are substances that are punctuated with the forms that together yield diversity requires the correlative assumption that such a diversity can only be sustained by these forms reinserting themselves in the wholes. Their reinserting themselves is just their self-development.

In the particular case of unity and kind, these requirements yield the following. Unity and kind are features of diversity that are natural to any whole. Being diversified by becoming a singular being of a certain kind is not a result of any external principle. But, if the essence of such a being is to ensure that it does not lapse back into a whole that is numerically undistinguished from other wholes and that is qualitatively undifferentiated from other wholes, then that essence must ensure the self-development of the being of that kind. At first, what the entity is is no more than a matter of promise, and this promise alone will not maintain the diversity within it.

The entity must realize the full potential of its kind. The response to the fundamental contradiction generated by the fundamental diversity between unity and kind is self-development.

This takes things back to the level of the quasi-articulate differences between the atomist and the complexist worldviews. But if it seems poetic to resort to the tension within wholes, what else is it to have to resort, as the atomist must, to a network of relations to combine simples? Ontology is forced back to a no-man's land between conceptionalization and myth to deal with fundamentals. There is where it emerges that change is inseparable from contradiction.

Down to Specifics

How is all of this about unity and kind related to the contradictions that dialecticians appeal to when dealing with a specific subject matter?

Hegel's contradictory pairs – slave and master, family and nation, morality and the world, object and consciousness – cannot be straight-jacketed as instances of unity and kind. Still, at the very rudimentary level of perceptual awareness there is, for Hegel, the contrast between the particularity of the presented object and the universality of the aspects under which it is taken. Beyond this, it is clear that however remote the workings of the dialectic at its various stages seem from the development of the contradiction between unity and kind, Hegel sees all of these workings as part of a process that ends by reconciling unity and kind, particular and universal in a wholeness that no longer allows for a tension between them. His mechanism for this reconciliation – self-consciousness – points his dialectic in an idealist direction that is purely accidental as far as a general dialectical ontology is concerned.

Marx's contradictory pairs are also ones that cannot be straight-jacketed as instances of unity and kind. The ones he is noted for are individual ownership and the collectivity of labour, increasing productivity and decreasing profitability, competitive exchange and increasing monopolization, use-value and exchange-value. Yet how are they to be fitted into the above scheme for dialectic? It is doubtless true that for

Marx, as for Hegel, there is a conflict due to complexity itself, even if for Marx it is resolved not by self-consciousness but by the destruction of the old and the formation of the new.[17] What must be shown is that the base contradiction involving unity and kind is the foundation for contradictions of a more specific nature.

The kind of an entity has to do with its promise to become something. But that promise may be realized in several ways, and thus it may be hard to recognize the kind to which an entity belongs simply by concentrating on the path of its essential development. For an entity to have determinateness in the course of the process of fulfilment, it also has distinguishing features or marks. In earlier logical discussions, distinguishing humans in terms of the *marks* of being featherless and having two feet was contrasted with characterizing humans as belonging to that *kind* of animal capable of rationality. Marks could distinguish one group of beings from another by reference to easily accessible features. But the specific difference of the kind was both less accessible and more basic in understanding the full range of behaviour in a group. In distinguishing marks from kind, we are building on this tradition. But emphasis is placed here, as it was not in that tradition, on the relational character of marks and on the character of marks as a substratum for the promise envisaged by the kind. Through its marks, the entity is assured of more than a purely isolated existence; it comes to stand in relation to other entities by the definiteness of its marks.[18] Its marks are the occurrent features it grounds relations to others in. This is not to imply that marks are accidental whereas the kind is essential. Both are manifestations of essence for both are internal differentiations of the entity itself.

The process implied by being in a kind is not just accidentally related to the having of marks. For, though the process of self-development implied by kind is internal in the sense of having an inner determinant it is not internal in the sense of taking place apart from the influence of other entities. To make possible this interaction the entity that develops must be determinate for other entities. And mere promise does not provide this determinateness. This determinateness is provided by the distinguishing features or marks. They are the determinate base for relations to other entities, which are in turn crucial for the process of self-development to continue.

The entity's first contradiction, arising from unity and kind, leads to its second contradiction, arising from kind and marks. This second contradiction is the first hint of concrete opposition, as opposed to the abstract opposition of multiplicity in unity. The reason for this is that, taken in isolation, kind and marks will imply incompatible courses of development. The actual course of development of an entity is a synthesis of these incompatible tendencies. This 'natural' contradiction does not involve negative terms as does logical contradiction. But it involves more than mere diversity within the substance of a whole. The duality of unity and kind does not involve a natural contradiction since unity does not imply a development at all, much less one incompatible with that of kind.

Plato gave an image of natural contradiction in the *Timaeus* where Reason and Blind Necessity or Chance were pitted against one another. Blind Necessity represents the tendencies of the marks entities have. Taken by themselves these tendencies would not lead to the full development of an entity of a given kind. For that, these tendencies must be harnessed by the tendencies of the kind itself. This is the overcoming of Blind Necessity by Reason.[19] Since the tendencies of the marks do not lead to the fulfilment of the kind but are harnessed by the tendencies of the kind, the marks have the character of a substratum of an entity.

The tendencies of the marks are ideal since of themselves they are not the full internal source of the changes an entity undergoes. But they are nonetheless real since they are a partial source of such changes.[20] The realization of the tendencies based on marks shows how the tendencies based on the kind have harnessed the marks to the purposes of the kind. Because of this the dialectical view cannot accept physicalism when formulated as the thesis that once the physical state of the system, such as one including persons, is specified the overall state of the system is uniquely determined. The difficulty is that the physical state *alone* does not determine anything about non-physical aspects of the system.

These aspects are determined only by a synthesis of marks and kind.

The non-dialectical materialist thinks that the marks or substratum can be 'uncoupled' from the kind and that deductions can be drawn from the marks so isolated. Advocates of the theory of the technological revolution make such an uncoupling of the forces of production from the social relations of production. The forces of production – understood not as a static aggregate of techniques, plant, and equipment but as the process of changing productivity due to changes in techniques, plant, and equipment – provide the distinguishing marks of the capitalist economy in regard to the feudal economy it replaced. The stagnation of productivity under feudalism was followed by its rapid growth under capitalism. The social relations of production – again understood not as static rules governing different essential roles in production but as the process of accumulation of capital – is the essential process that is the kind of the economic system. The theory of the technological revolution gives preeminence to growth of productivity through technological change in accounting for the salient features of late capitalism.

This uncoupling of marks from kind is, for the dialectician, the source of a number of mistakes. First, it is a clear fact that technology is not a self-supporting phenomenon. It develops in the context of a social purpose. Much of technological innovation of the post-World War II period has had to do with making it easier for managers to control labour. This is no accident; it is accounted for only on the assumption that the accumulation of capital by way of the exploitation of labour is the aim within which the development of technology takes place.

Second, the relation of capital to technology, each understood as a factor of production, is misunderstood. It is argued by the theory of technological revolution that, since capital investment has not increased as fast as technology has in the United States in this century, technology takes over from capital as the goal of the system.[21] Here the increase in technology is measured as the increase in productivity – output per person hour – attributable to changing equipment. And the conclusion that technology takes over from capital is supposed to mean that the goal of increasing productivity through advances in equipment supersedes the goal of accumulating capital. The basis for this conclusion is not so much the data as the assumption that uncoupling the two factors is legitimate. As uncoupled and hence as relatively independent contributors to production, it is indeed the relative rates of growth of the two that determines which is preeminent. But if they are not uncoupled, it is easy enough to interpret the data as saying that productivity has increased so fast precisely because, in this period, there would be stagnation in the growth of capital without big productivity increases. It is accumulation, and hence social relations, that are harnessing technology, and thus the forces of production.

Nonetheless, the overall process of production is not determined by either the social relations or the forces of production in isolation. The natural contradiction between the two is resolved by a synthesis of the two tendencies. The tendency towards increasing productivity is often slowed by the tendency towards accumulation. When unrestrained, the former tendency leads to economic crises that upset accumulation. Thus the converse is also true, that accumulation is slowed by increased productivity. Non-dialectical materialists have to regard any contradiction here as apparent only. For, in their view, technology and capital are simply independent influences on the process of production.

One Big Union

The previous section wraps up the positive exposition of dialectic; it is time now for a little fence mending in this and the final section.

Is dialectic inevitably monistic? There is a simple interpretation of the thesis of complexity that does indeed make it monistic. This is the *interdependence interpretation*. According to it, interdependence eliminates distinctness. Complexes of interdependent entities become genuine unities. This interpretation of the thesis of complexity has been made by dialecticians like Engels who do not go on to draw the monistic conclusion and by those like Lukacs, in his early-1920s period, who tend to regard the isolation of any entity from others as 'reification'[22]. This interpretation of the thesis of complexity is illegitimate. Yet it is quite natural in view of the atomist residue in the ontology of many dialecticians.

What is missed by the interdependence interpretation of dialectic is the vast difference between, on the one side, causal interaction among distinct entities and, on the other side, the interpenetration of different components of one and the same entity. The relation between a test charge and an external electrical field is vastly different from that between a single entity's unity and its kind. Yet dialecticians have often mistakenly taken themselves to be talking about the former rather than the latter kind of relation. This leaves them open to the quite legitimate charge that dialectic offers nothing different from existing ontology and methodology, which is held to be fully adequate to the task of dealing with causal interdependence. Also it makes plain that dialecticians have, unwittingly, been socialized into accepting one of the fundamental premises of the atomist ontology. This is the price for wishing to operate in the same world of discourse with established philosophy. That premise is the one relating causal inseparability and ontological sameness that was insisted upon by both Descartes and Hume. It is that whatever objects are separable are also distinguishable.[23] Hence where there is genuine interdependence, and thus inseparability, there is sameness.

The interpenetration of components of a single entity seems closest to causal interdependence when the interpenetration is based on the essence of the entity. And it is such an interpenetration that dialectic is primarily concerned with. The mark and the kind of an entity both reflect its essence. They interpenetrate – each is the same entity as the other and both are the same as the whole they characterize – not as a matter of accident, but because of what the entity is of itself. Still the difference is striking. A test charge interacts with the electrical field in which it is placed without it being true that the charge and the field must have been brought together. Once brought together, there is interdependence in the sense that the charge's motion results from the field and the field is modified by the presence of the charge in it. By contrast, the forces and the social relations of production in the current United States economy interpenetrate not because of a chance conjunction of the two in that economy but on the basis of the fact that both are expressions of that economy.

The argument for monism, when full, explicit, runs as follows:

(a) Dialectic tells us that all entities that exist in their own right are complex;
(b) Science tells us that any two entities are inter-dependent;
(c) [Atomist] ontology tells us that interdependent entities are the same;
(d) Hence there is only one entity and it is complex.

If in place of the premise (a), one had the other atomist dictum that entities that are one are not different, then one would have reached the conclusion that there is only one entity and it is simple. But rejecting this atomist dictum in favour of the thesis of complexity is no excuse for accepting the other atomist dictum, expressed in premise (c). What is called for is not going half-way to meet the atomist but a total break with atomism. Yet once (c) is rejected there is no obvious route from dialectic to monism. A pluralist dialectic, not in the political but in the ontological sense, then becomes consistent.

There is a twist that might save the monist argument. Entities have powers and these powers relate these entities to others. For example, a might be causally related to b on the basis of a power of a. Now here is the twist. Since being so related to b is a component of a, b will be a component of a. As such it will be the same as a! Assuming the powers of a relate it causally to all entities – premiss (b) –, it follows that that there is only one entity[24].

The fallacy in this argument has a general form. It is that if a has the relation R to b then a has R as a component and a has b as a component. But quite clearly this means that having R-to-b is being treated as a heap of two entities, R being one of them and b being the other. And there is no way under this treatment of explaining how it is that b is actually what is related to a by R. For b lies alongside R as a component like any of the other components of *a*, most of which are not related to *a* by *R*. So it must be concluded that having *R* to *b* in no way implies that *b* is a component of *a*. All that can be concluded is that *R*ing *b* is, as a unit, a component of *a*.

Having shown that a pluralist dialectic is consistent, it must be left for actual dialectical studies of various subject matters to establish which among the relevant entities are the ones that stand on their own. Such studies will not neglect interdependence, but they will avoid what, to reverse Whitehead's phrase, must be called the Fallacy of Misplaced Abstractness.[25] That is, they will not assume that attributing concreteness to entities short of the universe is a bestowal of concreteness on something that is really abstract in the sense of being only one side of a genuine concrete entity. For example, on the one side, individualism and its abuses can be corrected by emphasizing certain relations of interdependence. It is not necessary to treat individuals as moments in groups in order to understand that human nature has a social component. The dispositions of individuals often exist only because certain groups exist, but from this it cannot be concluded that individuals are abstractions from groups.[26] On the other side, though, it is important to see that dualism as regards mind and body is a deeper error than that of missing certain interdependencies. The mental and the corporeal are best seen as components of a complex unity. Dualism is a common instance of that other fallacy, the Fallacy of Misplaced Concreteness.

The Real Danger

The question of idealism cannot be solved here but it must at least be raised. The question comes up for dialectic in connection with the thesis of essence. Idealism posits an essence that is self-consciousness. This essence expresses itself in the natural contradiction between the features of being an object of consciousness and being a part of consciousness itself. This object – subject contradiction is resolved by the development of self-consciousness. For, with the development of full self-consciousness, the object of consciousness is recognized as consciousness itself. Since, for the idealist, it is of the nature of being to be self-conscious, there is no need for the destruction of being to overcome the contradiction. Self-consciousness by giving consciousness the status of object, dissolves the tension in the whole between subject and object.

But there is no reason to interpret the thesis of essence idealistically, at least not within the confines of the general ontology of dialectic. As far as this ontology is concerned, there may be many different kinds of essence. It is also compatible with the materialist interpretation of essence according to which there are no beings whose full essence is self-consciousness. It is then no accident that, in criticizing Hegel, Marx focused on Hegel's conception of the essence of humans[27]. For Hegel the human essence was self-consciousness whereas for Marx it was the free activity of a physical being.

The purpose of this section is not to attempt to formulate a materialist interpretation of the thesis of essence that would allow for the development of a materialist dialectic. It is the more modest one of extending the analysis of atomism by showing that, unlike general dialectic, it does have idealist consequences. This undercuts any claim that an atomist ontology can provide a coherent backdrop for historical materialism.

Atomism will be considered here in two forms. According to the first form, atomism views all entities as either themselves simples or as systems of externally related simples. The requirement of simplicity is here understood to exclude the possibility of an entity being composed not only by physical parts but also by other entities such as properties, dispositions, or natures. If there are properties, dispositions, or natures, they are entities external to physical ones, and are hence either classes of simples or transcendent forms.

The crucial question concerns the nature of laws governing simples. The basis for laws cannot be components of the simples they govern. How then can the behaviour of simples be lawlike at all? The model for any answer here must be the treatment of properties, dispositions, and natures given by the ontology of atomism. Thus the model must be one that involves externalities. Lawlike behaviour must be imposed on the simples in the physical domain from a source external to them. Their behaviour results from no dynamic within them but from the laws which are the patterns imposed on them.[28]

Laws are collectively, then, the Reason of the universe, and the physical simples are its obedient Matter. To make things manageably brief, there are two versions of this Reason of the universe. The older one sees this Reason, the set of laws, as the content of a demiurgic being's mind. The laws do not impose themselves, since they are external, and thus they need to be applied by such a demiurge. The newer version, more in keeping with modern sophistication but still fundamentally mythological, sees Reason as the content of the minds of human beings. The laws are the accumulated, but changing, wisdom of human beings throughout history. The validation of laws does not, on the newer version, depend on anything beyond the content of human experience. If that experience were all there was, the laws could still be valid.

But whether one takes the older or the newer version of laws as externalities, no account is given as to why the dumb simples should obey them. The simples even lack the internal disposition to submit to an external imposition. So Reason, external or historical, will have no sway over them. When this fact has sunk into the atomist tradition, the response is to forget the dumb simples. The simples are either transformed into the same stuff as laws or the simples disappear altogether and nothing is left but Reason, eternal or historical. The physical has disappeared and idealism results.

According to its second form, atomism views all entities as simples in the sense that they are exhausted by physical parts. There is nothing that is a component of any entity that is not a physical part. Protons, salt molecules, and blood cells can be components but qualities, dispositions, and natures cannot be. The requirement of simplicity is here understood to exclude the possibility of an entity being composed by properties, dispositions, and natures, but it does not exclude composition by physical parts.[29] There are two advantages to this form of atomism. First, it is not burdened with the view that there are smallest bits of matter, as the first form of atomism is. It admits a multiplicity of physical parts within a genuine unity, and in so doing accepts the dialecticians thesis of complexity. It merely puts limits on the kinds of entities that can enter into such a complexity. Second, it is not burdened with the view that plants, people and societies are mere aggregates of simples. They are, for it, genuine unities of multiple parts. As genuine unities, there can be laws about such entities. There can be no laws about such entities for the atomist who holds to the stronger requirement of simplicity that excludes physical complexity. For, laws must be about genuine entities.

The unity of multiple physical parts is just not enough. For, this second, or new, form of atomism is subject in the end to the same criticism as the first. And, of course, the difficulty has to do with the entities – properties, dispositions, natures – excluded from physical entities by even the weakened requirement of simplicity. The fastidious application of the principle of unities containing multiplicity that prevents properties and other entities from being included within the multiplicity gives the new atomism a serious handicap. This fastidiousness comes from a scientistic mentality. This mentality supposes that, if physical science analyses a whole into certain entities characteristic of physical science, there can be no other components of that whole which would play the role of its organizing principles and which would thus give it the status of a genuine unity. Curiously, though, this fastidiousness in regard to the internal structure of entities does not prevent a prodigality in regard to externalities. Scientism does not keep the new atomist from positing properties that are either forms or classes transcending physical entities. Nor does it keep the new atomist from having a structure of rationality – the set of laws – that is not constitutive of the physical things obeying these laws.

The problem of accounting for the fact that physical entities obey any laws arises as it did before. There is not the way out of saying that the whole is governed by a special law that is grounded in the way the parts combine. For, the way the parts combine is not itself something that can be internal to the entity, if indeed an entity is exhausted by its physical parts. (If the way the parts combine simply means the spatial configuration of the parts, rather than something amounting to a law itself, there is no reason why the way the parts, which themselves have no internal determination, combine should be the basis for a law for the whole.) One is then led to the mentalistic interpretation of law arrived at above. The laws of a physically complex whole are imposed on it by mind, eternal or historical. For, without a doubt the Reason of the universe, when it is not inherent in things as it is for dialectic, will make the universe rational only by the agency of a being with mental attributes. And once laws become mental, the things they govern will have to become mental too.

It is of interest that these tendencies of the new atomism have begun to be realized, even if only in sketchy and non-systematic ways. Quine has shown himself in this regard to have been one of the most persistent of the new atomists. He gives strong hints that physical entities must be drawn, along with laws, into the realm of the structure of historical mind.[30] The notion of ontological relativity has the function, for Quine, of reconciling the atomist to the idealist consequences of atomism. Laws are the creatures of theories and of background theories for these initial theories. They cannot be otherwise in a universe whose only internal structure is that of physical complexity. But then what can laws mean for these complex things? Nothing if the complexes are not themselves drawn into that very realm of theories and theoretical background.[31] Of course, background theories, relative to which the physical entities in given theories are meaningful, change. But this only means that it is not an eternal but only an historical mind that gives structure to, and ultimately being to, the universe of physical entities.

It is the absence of the thesis of essence in the new atomism that pushes it in the direction of idealism. Only when the multiplicity in a given unit is an expression of various aspects of that unit's essence is there any meaning at all to the idea that this unit develops after the pattern of a law. The contradiction of unity and multiplicity in the new atomism generates change not of itself but by bringing it within the realm of mind. The culture of present society with that society's need for an atomist outlook sets the stage for historical cycles beginning in atomism and ending in idealism. The foundations of any materialism that does not lead to an acceptance of idealism will have to be a dialectical ontology.

Notes

1 Karl Popper says that Marx's dialectics, like Hegel's, is a 'dangerous muddle' (*The Open Society and its Enemies*, II (New York 1967), p. 320).

2 Sidney Hook says science needs 'no special dialectic logic' ['Dialectic in society and history', in *Readings in Philosophy of Science*, Feigl and Brodbeck (eds.) (New York 1953), p. 708].

3 See the interpretation of internal strife as physical inhomogeneity by Mario Bunge, *Causality* (Cleveland 1963), p. 115.

4 Frederick Engels, *Anti-Dühring* (New York 1966), chaps. 12–13.

5 For an examination of the consequences of an ontology of complexes for some central issues in metaphysics, see Milton Fisk, *Nature and Necessity* (Bloomington 1973), chaps. 3, 7, 8, and 11. A defence of the 'essentialism' adopted here as an integral part of dialectic is given in chap. 2 of *Nature and Necessity*.

6 The idea of internal negation concerns differences within a unity and contracts with the idea of external negation that concerns both the numerical otherness and qualitative differences among distinct entities. For Hegel, essence is negative since through it a being becomes something for itself – it becomes a unity and develops as a member of a kind. See *Science of Logic*, II, Johnston and Struthers (trs.) (London 1951); I, bk. 2, sec. 1, chaps. 1–2, pp. 15–70.

7 Among neo-Marxists, Lucio Colletti adopts such a neo-Kantian approach to contradictions and tries to limit the external world to contrariety. 'Marxism and dialectic', *New Left Review*, 93 (Sept.–Oct. 1975), pp. 3–29.

8 Hegel, *Science of Logic*, II, Johnston and Struthers (trs.); I, bk. 2, sec. 1, chap. 2, C, pp. 58–62.

9 A representative passage is John Dewey, *Human Nature and Conduct* (New York 1930), pp. 127–8.

10 '... the whole of human science consists in this, that we have understanding of the manner in which those simple natures combine to compose other things'. Descartes, *Rules for the Guidance of Our Native Powers*, Rule XII; in *Descartes: Philosophical Writings*, N. K. Smith (tr.) (New York 1958), p. 65.

11 Locke had said that the real essence is that 'constitution of the parts of matter' on which the powers of the substance depend. *Essay Concerning Human Understanding*, Fraser (ed.) (New York 1959), II, bk. 3, chap. 6, sec. 6, pp. 61–2.

12 C. D. Broad, 'The relation between induction and probability, Part II', *Mind*, XXIX (1920), pp. 11–45.

13 'Identity is only the determination of the simple immediate, or of dead Being, while Contradiction is the root of all movement and life'. Hegel, *Science of Logic*, II, Johnston and Struthers (trs.), II, bk. 2, sec. 1, chap. 1, C, p. 67.

14 Hegel's treatment of identity is based on the Aristotelian distinction between sameness in the essential sense – sameness with an internal basis – and sameness in an accidental sense, stated in *Metaphysics*, Delta (1018a1–9). Hegel's discussion starts with a consideration of the manner in which essence leads to identity. *Science of Logic*, II, Johnston and Struthers (trs.), I, bk. 2, sec. 1, chap. 2, A, pp. 37–8.

15 'Singleness, therefore, makes its appearance there as true singleness, as the inherent nature of the "one", or as reflectedness into self. This is still, however, as conditioned self-existence alongside which appears another self-existence, the universality opposed to singleness and conditioned by it. But these two contradictory extremes are not merely alongside one another, but within one unity'. Hegel, *Phenomenology of Mind*, J. B. Baillie (tr.) (London 1949), A, II, p. 176.

16 Hegel says, 'It is an old proposition that One is Many, and more especially that the Many are One. We may here repeat the observation that the truth of the One and the Many, expressed in propositions, appears in an inadequate form; and that this truth can be seized and expressed only as a Becoming and as a process, as Repulsion and Attraction, and not as a Being; but it is as the latter, as a stable unity, that it is taken in a proposition'. *Science of Logic*, I, Johnston and Struthers (trs.), I, bk. 1, chap. 3, C, pp. 185–6.

17 Marx speaks of Hegel's '*false* positivism' when criticizing Hegel for making the negation of the negation into a 'confirmation' rather than an 'annulment' of the original negation. Karl Marx, 'Critique of the Hegelian dialectic and philosophy as a whole', in *The Economic and Philosophic Manuscripts of 1844*, in *The Marx-Engels Reader*, Robert C. Tucker (ed.) (New York 1972), pp. 96–8.

18 For Hegel on 'marks', see *Phenomenology of Mind*, Baillie (tr.), C, V, A, a, p. 286.

19 There is a fascinating discussion of this point in its relation to modern views of laws in Francis M. Cornford, *Plato's Cosmology* (Indianapolis, no date), pp. 161–76.

20 When Marx speaks of the law of the tendency of the rate of profit to fall, he is conscious that he is drawing out the consequences of only one of two aspects of the economic system of capitalism. That tendency represents the historical task of capitalism, which is to increase productivity, and it is pitted against the countervailing force of the limited purpose of capitalism, which is to accumulate capital. Karl Marx, *Capital*, III (New York 1967), pt. 3, chap. 13, pp. 212–13; chap. 15, sec. 2, pp. 249–50. This is a special case of the Hegelian doctrine of laws, according to which each law represents the tendency of one-side of a contradiction and thus does not fully represent the actual course of reality. *Science of Logic*, II, Johnston and Struthers (trs.), II, sec. 2, chap. 1, C, b, p. 364.

21 Daniel Bell, *The Coming of Post-industrial Society* (New York 1976), pp. 191–3.

22 This is the exaggerated theme of Georg Lukacs' masterful 'Reification and the consciousness of the proletariat', in *History and Class Consciousness*, (London 1971), pp. 83–222.

23 David Hume, *A Treatise of Human Nature*, Selby-Bigge (ed.) (Oxford 1951), bk. 1, pt. 1, sec. 7, p. 18.

24 This is the structure of Hegel's argument for monism, at the level of 'essence'. *Science of Logic*, II, Johnston and Struthers (trs.), I, bk. 2, sec. 3, chap. 3, B and C, pp. 191–205.

25 Alfred North Whitehead, *Science and the Modern World* (New York 1949), chap. 3, p. 52.

26 An ontology of groups is worked out by Milton Fisk in 'Society, class, and individual', *Radical Philosophers' Newsjournal*, II (March 1974), pp. 7–22.

27 Marx, 'Critique of the Hegelian dialectic and philosophy as a whole', in *The Marx-Engels Reader*, Tucker (ed.), pp. 90–3.

28 Leibniz, 'On nature in itself; or on the force residing in created things, and their actions', in *Leibniz: Selections* (ed.), Weiner (New York 1951), p. 142. The distinction drawn by Leibniz is that between laws as 'extrinsic denominations' and 'indwelling' laws.

29 For an elegant development of this new atomism see G. P. Hellman and F. W. Thompson, 'Physicalism: ontology, determination, and reduction', *Journal of Philosophy*, 72 (1975), pp. 551–64.

30 W. V. Quine, *Ontological Relativity and Other Essays* (New York 1969), p. 51. The key idea is expressed in the following passage: 'Such talk of subordinate theories and their ontologies *is* meaningful, but only relative to the background theory with its own primitively adopted and ultimately inscrutable ontology'.

31 Lenin refers approvingly to Feuerbach for the idea that any ontology which is unable to regard laws as internal to the world of physical things must end by bringing those things into the same mental realm as the laws themselves are relegated to. 'With Feuerbach the recognition of objective law in nature is inseparably connected with the recognition of the objective reality of the external world, of objects, bodies, things, reflected by our mind. . . . For it is, indeed, clear that the subjectivist line on the question of causality, the deduction of the order and necessity of nature not from the external objective world, but from consciousness, reason, logic, and so forth, not only cuts human reason off from nature, not only opposes the former to the latter, but makes nature a *part* of reason, instead of regarding reason as a part of nature' Lenin, *Materialism and Empirio-Criticism*, in *Collected Works*, XIV (Moscow 1972), p. 155.

5 *From the* Grundrisse *to* Capital: *The Making of Marx's Method*

JOHN MEPHAM

I

THIS essay started life as a response to reading Rosdolsky's *The Making of Marx's 'Capital'*.[1] The ostensible problems dealt with by Rosdolsky in his book, and by myself in my critique of it, are problems about Marx's method, about the Hegelian substance of this method, and about the *Grundrisse* as a text to which we might turn in seeking to understand the method of *Capital*. These problems are also dealt with at length by other authors in this present volume. But it turned out that hiding behind this manifest discussion was another, and for me more worrying problem: that is the problem of *reading*. It turned out that evaluating Rosdolsky's views involved thinking about his method of reading, and about my method of reading: in fact it raised the question of whether reading is a methodical process at all.

Reading is a difficult and sometimes unnerving activity. This is especially true if one is reading the work of an author for whom one has respect and admiration and yet with whom one has deep differences of opinion. This was the case in my reading of Rosdolsky. I came to believe that he had approached Marx's texts with facile presuppositions about their unity and transparency. But in coming to believe this I was myself perhaps approaching Rosdolsky's text with similarly facile presuppositions. Whether or not this was so, what I want to emphasize is that when philosophers read Marx and Engels with certain investigations in mind a rather obscure interchange takes place. We ask Marx and Engels certain questions about method, about Hegel, about dialectics, and we hunt among their writings for answers. In the present case Rosdolsky emerged with certain answers, and I emerged with others. This was both because we took certain differences with us into our readings, but also because we read differently. This is why I am concerned here not so much to directly defend my own views (they are more or less simply announced rather than systematically argued for) as to demonstrate (in the same sense that a biochemist might 'demonstrate' an experiment) the process of reading which in part produced them.

There is a certain kind of 'scholarly' way of reading of Marx (or of anybody else for that matter) which is unlike that which I have in mind. This kind of scholarly way of reading is like a histological examination of fine structure, in which an unproblematic instrument, the microscope, is employed in the investigation of an organism. But it involves at least two presuppositions: the instrument as a tool of investigation, and the idea that the object of investigation is like an organism, that it has a certain kind of anatomical and physiological unity, that is that it can, as we say, be construed as a 'totality'. But what I wish to convey about reading is that, while it certainly should pay attention to fine detail, and involve sensitivity to tiny clues, it should also contain a recognition of just how little like an autonomous and functionally fully competent organism a text can really be.

Apart from different ways of reading there are also different readers. Different readers have different frameworks of assumptions. Rosdolsky comes to Marx's *Grundrisse* and to *Capital* as a classical Marxist, and also as an exile living in a certain historical and cultural situation. He reads in Marx, or into him, a view about the central importance in his work of Hegelian dialectical method. He locates the clues that identify this method for us in the *Grundrisse*. I, on the other hand, come to Rosdolsky armed against him. I have certain views of my own: that there is a profound difference between speculative, or metaphysical, discourse and the discourses of the sciences; that Marx's method is dialectical but that we do not know very well what this means in spite of the vast literature on the subject. I also have certain suspicions: I am suspicious of certain views about how books come to be written, how texts come to be produced, views which are so 'obvious' that they must be wrong. I also adopt certain

rules in reading: watch out for the metaphors, listen for the
passages where the emotional investment breaks through
into the open, never forget that writing is not like speaking,
that it involves scissors and paste. What follows could itself
be read with such rules in mind.

II

Roman Rosdolsky (1898–1967) was born in Lvov and was
among the founders of the Communist Party of the Western
Ukraine.[2] He was by training a historian. Politically he
became a Trotskyist. His theoretical commitment to classical
Marxism and his political stand against Stalin made of him a
member of a diminishing band of East European intellectuals,
caught between the barbarisms of East and West, very few of
whom were to survive these grotesque turns of European
history. During the war Rosdolsky was captured by the
German army, but he survived the concentration camps and
in 1945 he emigrated to the USA. There he lived in isolation,
pursuing his historical and theoretical research. His situation
was thus one of more or less complete geographical and
cultural separation from the tradition of Marxist theory and
politics with which he identified and which had been all but
swept from the stage of history, surviving only precariously
in the efforts of a few intellectuals such as Isaac Deutscher and
Rosdolsky himself.

In the West Marxism had retreated into academic, metaphysical obscurantism, and in the East it had been replaced by
vulgar Stalinist philistinism. Rosdolsky therefore saw himself as having a historical mission – he wanted, in the most
difficult and seemingly hopeless circumstances, to maintain
contact with that tradition of classical Marxism that had
flourished in the early decades of the century, to keep intact
its fragile historical continuity and to help to prepare for its
revival. So in writing *The Making of Marx's 'Capital'* he had
definite objectives in mind. As he says in his Preface:

> I am, by profession, neither an economist nor a philosopher. I would
> not have dared to write a commentary on the *Rough Draft* [*Grund-*

risse] if a school of Marxist theoreticians still existed today – as it did in the first thirty years of this century – which would have been better equipped to carry out this task. However, the last generation of notable Marxist theoreticians for the most part fell victim to Hitler's and Stalin's terror, which interrupted the further development of the body of Marxist ideas for several decades.

Rosdolsky believed that the biggest obstacle to revitalizing Marxist economic thought was lack of understanding of Marx's method. The main problem was to grasp the logic of *Capital*. The strange thing is, however, that instead of turning directly to *Capital* Rosdolsky saw it as necessary to make a detour via a reading of the *Grundrisse*. For this latter text is richer in explicit methodological remarks than is *Capital* itself. In Rosdolsky's view, one can study in the *Grundrisse* the grand theoretical edifice of *Capital* in the process of its construction: one can read the history of its genesis (its *Entstehungsgeschichte* - as the German title of Rosdolsky's book puts it).

In terms of his aim of contributing to the revival of Marxist economic thought Rosdolsky's effort was a success, to the extent that his work has in fact contributed to this process in an important way, not only in Germany but also in the international Trotskyist movement (via the work of Mandel) and in Great Britain (via his influence on the so-called Capital Logic school). Although the book has been influential, it suffers from serious theoretical and methodological weakness.

III

Why did Rosdolsky believe that the way to an understanding of the method of *Capital* was via a reading of the *Grundrisse*? Why not study *Capital* itself? There was, and indeed still is, no major commentary on *Capital*.[3] There is a clear need for a book in which the argument of *Capital* is dissected in detail, its logical and conceptual structure clearly exposed, and its textual history analyzed. A book such as Rubin's *Essays on Marx's Theory of Value*[4] (another text written by one of that lost generation of classical Marxists, in this case by a victim of

Stalinism) demonstrates the usefulness of this kind of work; but Rubin's book is incomplete and unsystematic (it deals only with parts of Volume I of *Capital* and that in a rather fragmentary way) and a more ambitious and sustained commentary would be invaluable. Rosdolsky is right in that that the most disputed aspects of *Capital* (the epistemological status of the concept of value, the alleged contradictions between Volumes I and III, the transformation problem, the reproduction schema, the falling rate of profit, the notion of a tendential law, etc.) all raise deep questions concerning Marx's method and require an understanding of scientific abstraction, the relation between abstract and concrete concepts, the development of categories, and so on. But why cannot these problems be addressed directly to *Capital* itself?

In Rosdolsky's view the general logical structure of *Capital* has often been misunderstood. This is in part because its principal structural feature, the development from abstract to concrete categories, is not explicitly discussed by Marx in Volume I, and more generally because its Hegelian method is left throughout more or less implicit. As for the first point Rosdolsky's main claim is that reading the *Grundrisse* reveals that Volumes I and II of *Capital* deal only with the analysis of '*capital in general*' whereas Volume III approaches the analysis of '*capital in concrete reality*'.

> When the young Lenin wrote his treatise on the realization problem neither Marx's *Theories* nor the *Grundrisse* were known to him: he could have had only a less than adequate insight into the methodologically very complex structure of Marx's economic work. We now know that according to Marx's plan for the structure of the work, the first two volumes only figure as the analysis of '*capital in general*' and that consequently the results which Marx obtained in these volumes – although extraordinarily important – still had to be concretised and supplemented by a later stage of the analysis, that of '*capital in concrete reality*'. The early Marxists, including Lenin, understandably overlooked this. (p. 481)

However, Rosdolsky's use of this distinction is very limited. He takes it simply as a matter of differences in the level of abstraction (or as the difference between abstract and concrete, as in the passage quoted above), but does not investigate in detail just what is involved in the procedure of scientific abstraction (as distinct, for example, from speculative philosophical abstraction) nor discuss in detail the specific application of these procedures in the text of *Capital* itself. In fact when explaining the distinction when it is first invoked (p. 46) he confuses it with a quite different distinction, namely that between aggregate capital and individual capital.

The concept of capital, of capital as such, as a specific social relation, is an abstract concept designating in part whatever is specific to any individual capital qua capital. It is, as Marx says (cited in Rosdolsky, p.47): 'an abstraction which grasps the specific differences which distinguish capital from other forms of wealth ... These are the features common to *each capital as such* or which make every specific sum of values into capital' (emphasis added). The concept of capital is necessarily the concept of a form of social wealth in which the means of production are divided into individual units which stand in a relation of competition with one another – that is 'competition in general', competition conceived abstractly. The derivation of the law of capitalist accumulation, for example, involves the abstract concept of competition that is conceived as yet without reference to the developed categories of profit, interest, etc., and without consideration of the division of the economy into specific departments and branches, and so on). This abstract law is expressed concretely in a particular way: 'competition subordinates every individual capitalist to the immanent laws of capitalist production, as external and coercive laws. It compels him to keep extending his capital, so as to preserve it, and he can only extend it by means of progressive accumulation' (*Capital*, Vol. I, p. 739).[5]

To point out that capital in general, capital as a specific form of social relation, is the object of investigation of *Capital*, Volume I, does not in itself get us very far. For we also need a detailed analysis of the relations between this concept and other concepts (value, competition, accumulation, and so on) and of the proof procedures whereby the laws and tendencies of the capitalist mode of production are derived from these concepts. This analysis is not provided by

Rosdolsky, whose discussion of Marx's method of abstraction is no more than preliminary. So whereas there is no doubt some truth in his claim (p. 51) that 'the categories "capital in general" and "many capitals" provide the key to the understanding of not only the *Rough Draft*, but also the later work, that is, *Capital*', his own exposition of these categories is too limited to be of much help in relation to fundamental problems of interpretation of *Capital*.

IV

For Rosdolsky, then, *Capital* suffers from the apparent 'abstruseness of its method of presentation' (p. 118), and this leaves it open to being read as a 'contrived metaphysical construction' (p.119). His general theme is that it is necessary to understand Marx's method of abstraction, so that what may appear metaphysical can be seen to be in fact 'realistic'. Unfortunately, his reading of *Capital* in the light of the *Grundrisse* is based on three quite unacceptable assumptions. As a result, Marx's method of abstraction is obscured by Rosdolsky's method of reading.

His first assumption is that the *Grundrisse* and *Capital* are identical as far as method is concerned:

> The main aim of this work has been of a methodological nature. We set out from the position that previous research was excessively concerned with the material content of Marx's economic work, and exhibited far too little interest in his specific method of investigation. We therefore tried to show how much the *Rough Draft* has to teach on the subject of methodology. (p. 445)

This method of investigation is said to be not metaphysical but, on the contrary, Hegelian. This startling thought runs throughout the book and the 'Hegelian inheritance of Marx's thought' (p. 492) is in fact its central theme.

> If Hegel's influence on Marx's *Capital* can be seen explicitly only in a few footnotes, the *Rough Draft* must be designated as a massive reference to Hegel, in particular to his *Logic* – irrespective of how radically and materialistically Hegel was inverted! The

publication of the *Grundrisse* means that academic critics of Marx will no longer be able to write without first having studied his method and its relation to Hegel. (p. xiii)

Rosdolsky's second assumption, a corollary of the first, is that *Capital* constitutes a unified, homogeneous discourse; that it is methodologically and theoretically without internal fissures and contradictions, so that there is a unique answer to the question of whether or not it is in some sense methodologically Hegelian. The implication of this is, in effect, that *Capital* cannot be subjected to *critical* analysis. For example, Rosdolsky cannot pose the question of whether the history of conflicting interpretations of *Capital* and of reconstructions of its argument might be in part a result of its own internal discrepancies. Perhaps some sections of *Capital*, or some of its concepts, are after all 'metaphysical contrivances'.

Rosdolsky's third assumption is that two discourses, one philosophical and the other economic, can be *conceptually identical* and differ only in their *manner of presentation*: in other words that the manner of presentation is 'conceptually neutral'. The bulk of his exposition of the content of the *Grundrisse* in fact comes down to this, that each section is identified as corresponding to some section of *Capital*, and their manifest differences are dismissed as superficial. 'The distinction lies chiefly in the manner of presentation' (p. 203).

Over and above differences of presentation there are, on Rosdolsky's view, other differences between the two texts, but they are not differences of essential conceptual content or method. On this view the concepts in the *Grundrisse* are the same as those in *Capital* but in an as yet less refined state. The *Grundrisse* represents a stage in the development of *Capital*, but the development involved is implicitly perceived as a continuous and unilinear process.

> ... the *Rough Draft* differs considerably ... from Volume I of *Capital*. The *Rough Draft* lacks not only the strict conceptual distinctions ... in addition the mode of presentation itself has an abstract character and exhibits traces of a 'coquetting with the Hegelian mode of expression'. In fact, though, the results of the analysis are the same in both texts ... [The *Rough Draft* is] Marx's

scientific workshop, and allows us to witness the process by which his economic theory develops. (p. 210)

The problem, however, is whether or not this essentially teleological view of the matter does not misrepresent the process of development of Marx's thought. A set of metaphors, familiar enough from the works of 'historians of ideas', can create a teleological illusion. An earlier text is perceived as the *origin* of a later text, or as stage in its *development*, as the latter *in statu nascendi :* the elements of the latter are said to be present in the former, but as yet in an unrefined state, as yet without clear exposition, and so on.

In fact, however, the process of production of the later text may actually have involved a shift, a displacement, a radical discontinuity with some discourse or discourses which are effective and dominant in the earlier text. Invoking these metaphors involves understanding the process of production of a text as a process of struggle rather than one of development: and in the case we are discussing it involves understanding the process of production of *Capital* as one in which there was a struggle to release discourse from the dominance of Hegelian methods and categories. Rosdolsky's method of reading prevents him from coming to terms with this possibility. For an evaluation of these alternative views of the matter is only possible on the basis of a detailed analysis of the texts concerned. If a text is the site of play of conflicting discourses, this can be revealed by examining it not just in relation to the 'results' at which it arrives (which is Rosdolsky's method) but in relation to its concepts, objects of investigation, problems, metaphors, proof procedures, and so on. Since on Rosdolsky's assumption the *Grundrisse* is the origin of *Capital*, and *Capital* is the truth or *telos* of the *Grundrisse*, this allows him to dispel any obscurities in the earlier text by referring to the later text: his method often amounts to giving an exposition of the *Grundrisse* based on quotations from *Capital* and from *Theories of Surplus Value*. The fact that many sections of the *Grundrisse* are clearly philosophical or speculative in character does not therefore prevent him from identifying them with 'corresponding' sections, of a clearly economic character, in *Capital*.

In summary then, Rosdolsky's method is based on the assumption that *Capital* is a theoretically and methodologically unified text; it is blind to the text's internal fissures and discontinuities and to the effects in it of contradictory discourses: and it is based on the assumption that *Capital* is the teleological end product of a process of development, and that its earlier prototypes, while rough, were nevertheless constructed from basically the same materials and on the same general plan. The anatomy of *Capital* is the key to the anatomy of the *Grundrisse*.

V

As an example of Rosdolsky's method of reading based on these assumptions we can look at his discussion of fetishism (pp. 123–9). He starts by giving an exposition of the concept of fetishism as it is to be found in the famous section 4 of Chapter 1 of *Capital*, 'The Fetishism of the Commodity and its Secret', because it is here that the analysis of the value-form 'provides the proof that the "riddle of the money fetish" is in fact "simply the riddle of the commodity fetish, now become visible and dazzling to our eyes"' (p. 126). But he warns us not to be misled by the fact that we can find in this section of *Capital*, *and nowhere else*, a 'proof' which connects together an analysis of the value-form, money and the commodity with the concept of fetishism, into believing 'that Marx's famous concept of "commodity fetishism" was first developed in the mid-1860s. It was already in evidence in his earliest economic works'. He cites, as an example, Marx's notes on Mill of 1844. In the long quotation from this early work provided by Rosdolsky there is no mention of *fetishism* at all; what is there is the notion of *alienation*. Rosdolsky takes these to be the same thing. He sums up his views on the matter by saying that 'All the elements of the later theory of commodity are already present here [in the 1844 notes], even if they appear *in philosophical guise*'. The '*real economic basis*' of the theory was to be provided only in *Capital*, although '*a foundation*' for it is to be found already in the *Grundrisse* (p. 128, emphases added).

In short, Rosdolsky expounds but does not criticize the concept of fetishism as it appears in that section of *Capital* : he assumes that this is a coherent, unified discourse. Secondly, he points to earlier texts, as if by a procedure of ostensive demonstration to show that the elements of this concept are to be found there. Thirdly, he notes that these elements are present there as the elements of a *philosophical* concept: or rather that philosophy acts simply as the guise, the mask which clothes the concept at that early point in its life, a mask which can simply be replaced or discarded on other occasions as the concept, the very same concept, is introduced into new company at different points in its career. When, older and more experienced, it mixes with the concepts of Marx's mature critique of political economy, it at last receives not only new clothes to wear but also a new name, 'fetishism', this belated baptism registering the fact that it has, one might be relieved to hear, also at last been provided with a 'foundation' and then 'a real basis' in economics. This strange compound of assumptions and metaphors deserves more careful scrutiny.

Do the passages from the 1844 notes on Mill which Rosdolsky quotes really reveal a conceptual continuity between the concept of alienation and that of fetishism? The question requires a longer and more detailed analysis than is possible here,[6] but the following brief points might be useful. The 1844 text is about forms of social mediation, and it is based on a contrast between two polar opposite forms: between mediation which is *exteriorized* and that which is *human*. Exteriorized mediation entirely negates human being – for man becomes 'exiled and dehumanized', 'his will, his activity, and his relations to others' are taken away from him and he exists entirely in a form of slavery to the real god of money, which is 'the real power' governing relations between men. On this view of 'alienated' social life the agency which governs social processes, that which effectively determines the course of social life, is an alienated intermediary, money. The agency is not, as it is in *Capital*, the relations between classes, class struggles, the relations of production, the tendential laws of development of the capitalist mode of production, and so on. The alienated intermediary, money, is not conceived as a consequence of the relations of production, of the forms of socialization of labour, but as itself the cause or basic principle governing social life. As Marx says explicitly in the passage quoted by Rosdolsky, value *'formed the basis* of the alienation of private property' and 'money is the sensuous, objective existence of this alienation' (p. 128, emphasis added). This conceptualization is entirely the *inverse* of that involved in *Capital;* the order of causality is upside down. It constitutes, from the point of view of the discourse of *Capital*, a *case of fetishism*, that is a theoretical ideology in which the order of determination is inverted and in which causal agency is misplaced onto the concrete. So the philosophical concept of alienation, far from being identical with that of fetishism, is rather an example of it.

So on one side of the polarity we have the alienated intermediary, money, and men are only pawns in its game, dehumanized and without power. On the other side of the polarity we have the suggestion that *'man himself* should be the intermediary between men' and the implication that those who exchange should 'relate to each other *as people*' (p. 127, emphases added). All this sounds reasonable enough unless one asks, what is this 'man himself', with its curious syntactical combination of a generality with a personal pronoun; and what is contained in the notion of relating to each other *as people*? For masters and slaves relate to each other as people (in ways which are specifically different from the way they relate to dogs and trees; for example, they talk to each other, give orders, love and hate, and so on). The phrases 'man himself' and 'as people' implicitly trade on some *untheorized* ideal of the *really human*, some vision of *true humanity* being expressed in social life. They are functioning as metaphors in which idealized relations between *individuals* are illicitly mapped onto a utopian scheme of patterns of relations in general, relations in which social organizations (political organizations, institutions, collectivities of all kinds) have entirely disappeared. The disjunction between 'the human' and 'the dehumanized', as forms of social mediation, is empty of cognitive content, for the valorization of the former is based on nothing more than an implicit, essentialist and individualist philosophical imperative. What is basically an ethical distinction between the 'human' and the 'dehumanized' is not objectionable in itself. What is objectionable is that in this discourse it pretends to some other status, for it slides surreptitiously into an allegedly explanatory discourse in which basic agencies determining the course of social life are purportedly identified. There is no conceptual linkage between these figures and a theory of the social relations of production, nor with theories about human capacities and powers (linguistics, psychoanalysis, theories of perception, and so on). The space which should be occupied (and which in *Capital* is occupied) by theoretical discourse concerning the various forms taken by human societies through historical development, is entirely occluded by a simple philosophical/ethical polarity with no explanatory power.

The concept of fetishism, on the other hand, is rooted in the problematic of Marx's critique of political economy. It is linked with the concept of the socialization of labour and its various forms, and with the analysis of the value-form, money and the commodity. Within this general problematic the concept of fetishism has primarily an epistemological significance, that is it does not designate, as does the concept of alienation, some generalized dehumanization of man, but refers to the specific effects of the capitalist relations of production on the ways in which social life tends to be represented. In saying all of this I am *contrasting* the figures of alienation and of fetishism (whereas Rosdolsky assimilates them) without actually *endorsing* the latter. I am not presupposing that fetishism is an unproblematic, fully coherent theoretical concept. As an epistemological concept it is ambiguous. The text invites us to read it either as part of a *general* theory of ideology, of the production of misleading representations throughout the culture which is secreted by bourgeois society, or as a much less ambitious concept, limited to functioning within the critique of a specific theoretical ideology, that of political economy.[7] This is not the place to attempt an evaluation of the concept: my point is only that Rosdolsky should have subjected it to criticism. I am using it as an example of his persistent tendency to take *Capital* to be a coherent, unified text.[8]

I should also emphasize that I am not contrasting ethical or normative discourse with scientific or theoretical discourse in order to damn the former and embrace the latter. I am pointing to a *problem*, that of the relations between these discourses. In the passages from the Notes on Mill under discussion the ethical polarities seem to float free of any anchorage in a theoretical representation of social life; or rather they are located within a philosophical discourse which makes such an anchorage impossible. Normative discourse does indeed also pervade *Capital*. Thinking about social life normatively is not in itself a juvenile delinquency of which the 'young Marx' has to be found guilty and the 'old Marx' acquitted (though there is a tendency among those influenced in the wrong way by Althusser to talk as if this were so). If there is an epistemological break in Marx's work it is not one which results in the elimination of normative discourse. The problem, however, is to investigate the *relation* between the normative and the theoretical in Marx's different works, or more generally to investigate the different functions and effects of the normative in different kinds of discourse. In *Capital*, for example, not only the section on the fetishism of commodities, but more especially the short Chapter 13, 'On Cooperation', is thoroughly imbued with normative considerations, and is perhaps the part of *Capital* which is closest in its argument to the sections of the *Economic and Philosophical Manuscripts of 1844* on alienation. A systematic comparative reading of these texts would be extremely useful. More expansively, the whole of Part 4 of *Capital*, 'Production of Relative Surplus-Value', is built around the fusion between the theory of surplus-value and of the labour-process with the development of machinery and modern industry on the one hand, and normative considerations on the other. These latter can be summarized by saying that, for Marx, knowledge of societies and of nature, control over the forces determining human lives, and the satisfaction of historically developed human needs, are ends in themselves, and that there are certain historically specific potentialities for their development, and historically specific barriers to their development, within the capitalist mode of production. Theoretical understanding of the capitalist mode of production and of its tendential laws is an essential component of strategic, practical thought and activity which aims through struggle to actualize a society in which there is space for the emergence of *the fully developed individual* (*the* central normative concept in Marx's thought). These normative themes, which are of course to be found even more explicitly developed in parts of the *Grundrisse*, stand in a certain relation to the cognitive themes which are dominant in *Capital*. The question is, what is this relation?

VI

Now to examine further how in other instances Rosdolsky's assumptions and methods of reading work out when tested against the texts themselves, by looking in some detail at Rosdolsky's reading of them. A clear case in which it would be a serious mistake to *assume* that the text of *Capital* constitutes a unified theoretical discourse is the discussion of the value-form and of money in Part I of Volume I. In these sections there seem to coexist at least two mutually incompatible discourses (with different problematics, different proof procedures and different theorems). The sections on the value-form have been reconstructed by commentators in two main ways: there are two competing accounts of the proof procedure involved in relation to the labour theory of value (Chapter 1, Section 1). On the one hand there is the view that the proof procedure is a *formal* one, that is that it is a matter of 'determination of concepts'. On this view the relation between labour time and value is derived from a consideration of the logic of the commensuration involved in the relative numerical scale of exchangeability of commodities. According to this interpretation the argument seeks to *prove* that value is a measure of abstract labour time, on the basis of an analysis of the *concept* of value and the *logic* of the value-form. For some this proof procedure is Hegelian (see, for example, the views of Stanley Moore, discussed by Chris Arthur in this present volume) and is an example of metaphysical abstraction (looking for the common commensurable property shared by all commodities by virtue of which they all fall under this abstract concept), though it seems to me more accurate to characterize the proof as a Kantian transcendental one, in which the common property is derived as a necessary condition for inter-commensurability. In either case the form of abstraction involved would be philosophical and not scientific, and the argument would in fact be invalid even according to the protocols governing proof procedures in this kind of argument, since labour time is not in fact the unique common property of commodities which could serve as the basis for their numerical exchangeability (utility is another possibility). Therefore the relation between value and labour time cannot be demonstrated by formal or conceptual analysis.

According to the second interpretation (see, for example, Rubin's *Essay on Marx's Theory of Value*) Marx was aware that the question of what value is the measure of can only be answered by reference to non-formal considerations concerning the process of socialization of labour in a society in which products take the form of commodities, that is by reference to what, he calls the 'process of social metabolism'. Thus the text is not to be read as providing a formal, conceptual proof of the labour theory of value but, on the contrary, as *assuming* the law of value as the mechanism for the allocation of labour to the different branches of production, and on this basis deriving an analysis of the forms which are the necessary consequence. In other words the argument would go *from* an analysis of social relations *to* an analysis of forms. The proof procedure involved here would be quite different from that discussed above, since it would be based on an analysis of the real consequences of real social relations, and this analysis would underlie the analysis of concepts and forms. The abstraction of the concept of value would thus also have a quite different status: it would be, as Marx says, a 'real abstraction', one which was the product not of philosophical speculation but of real social processes.

There is plenty of biographical information to support the view that Marx himself would have accepted this second interpretation. But it should not be assumed that only one or other of these interpretations is correct, for the text itself is ambiguous. In fact Marx had great difficulty in drafting the section in *Capital* on the value-form. The first edition was published with an 'Appendix on the Value-Form' which Marx added because of his (and Engel's) dissatisfaction with his exposition in the main text. For later editions he thoroughly reworked what was to become Section 3 of Chapter 1. After the publication of *Capital* he found that it was frequently being read in ways which he took to be complete misinterpretations of his argument (it was read along the lines of the first interpretation above). On Marx's view of the matter his exposition does not start with concepts but with real relations: 'The unfortunate fellow does not see that even if there were no chapter on "value" at all in my book, the analysis of the real relations which I give would contain the proof and demonstration of the real value relation.' (Cited by Rosdolsky, p. 97). But these various facts give indirect support to the view that the text itself is discursively heterogeneous, that Marx had not succeeded in removing the discrepancy between his subjective intentions and the actual exposition. For there do remain sections of the text in which the discourse of social relations is submerged beneath the philosophical discourse on 'common properties' and formal contradictions.

In *Capital* as a whole it is the discourse on social relations which is dominant. Those such as Rubin who read the early sections of *Capital* along the lines of the second interpretation above, are quite right in insisting that this reading is supported by the overall argument of the book. But it is significant that in giving an exposition of the theory of value Rubin (and also Rosdolsky) does not, in fact cannot, follow in detail the line of argument in the text itself, but relies instead on a very selective reading of the text supported by reference to Marx's correspondence and other ephemeral writings. When Rosdolsky attempts (p. 119) to defend the view that Marx's theory of value is not a 'contrived metaphysical construction' he cannot do so by examining Chapter I of *Capital* itself (nor by reference to the *Grundrisse*): rather, he draws on and quotes from *Capital* Volume III, *Wage-Labour and Capital* and Hilferding's *Das Finanzkapital*, as if it could be safely assumed that these various texts are all coherent both with each other and with the relevant sections of *Capital* Volume I. But this method of exposition, which Rosdolsky employs throughout his book, makes any serious examination of the issues impossible.

As for the *Grundrisse*, there is no section in it corresponding to Chapter 1 of *Capital*. As Rosdolsky points out (p. 97) whereas 'there is no presentation of the theory of value in the *Rough Draft*', the whole argument of this text is implicitly based on it, that is it is present as an *assumption*. The *Grundrisse* starts not with the commodity and the value-form but with money, and specifically with a critique of Proudhon's labour-money theory. The focus in this critique is immediately on forms of socialization of labour, and the direction of the proof is from the relations of production to money conceived as a consequence of these. Marx demonstrates that to reform money without changing the relations of production, as was proposed by the Proudhonists, is to 'attack consequences whose causes remain unaffected'.

Having developed this discourse of social relations and 'the social nexus' (in passages on pp. 136–65 of the *Grundrisse*[9]), Marx then reverts to a thoroughly Hegelian discussion of 'the transition from value to money' in which, as Marx himself realized, merely formal argument comes to the fore and displaces the procedures which had been effective in the earlier critique of Proudhon. Rosdolsky correctly notes the Hegelian character of these sections of the *Grundrisse* but he does not recognize the incompatibility between these utterly different forms of argument. Rather he sees the problem simply as a matter of Marx's struggling to discover a manner of presentation which will make his argument appear less 'contrived'. However, the problem with speculative method is not simply that it appears to the simple-minded reader as contrived but that it is in fact thoroughly inadequate as a form of scientific explanation of social processes. In brief, it is idealist. Rosdolsky, both here and throughout the book, fails to register this fact.

> So much then on the dialectical derivation of money from value as it exists in the *Rough Draft*. To the reader who is not acquainted with Marx's theory this derivation might appear 'contrived' – an example of an empty 'dialectic of concepts', which endows economic categories with a life of their own, and, in truly Hegelian fashion, lets them originate from and pass over into one another. One interesting

incidental remark in the *Rough Draft* illustrates how easily such an impression can arise, and also shows that Marx himself allowed for the possibility of such a misinterpretation. He writes: 'It will be necessary later, before this question is dropped, to correct the idealist manner of its presentation, which makes it seem as if it were merely a matter of conceptual determinations and of the dialectic of these concepts' (p. 114).

Such a comment by Marx should indicate the need not for a Hegelian reading of *Capital* as performed by Rosdolsky, but rather for a direct attack on the problem of the difference between idealist and materialist argument, between philosophical speculation and scientific demonstration. A critical reading of the *Grundrisse* and of *Capital* is not possible if these differences are not clarified.

VII

Rosdolsky's methods of reading could be illustrated by reference to any number of examples. One of the most startling concerns the section of the *Grundrisse* on the development of capital out of money and the 'corresponding' section in *Capital*, Volume I, Part 2: these are discussed by Rosdolsky in Chapter 11 of his book. On Rosdolsky's view these two texts present *the same solution to the same problem* (p. 189): the only difference is that in *Capital*

> the solution is present in its finished form, with the intermediary stages left out, whereas here [in the *Rough Draft*] we can observe it, as it were, *in statu nascendi* ... It would therefore be pointless to counterpose the later, 'more realistic' seeming version of the solution in *Capital* to the more 'metaphysical' one in the *Rough Draft*. Both are the product of Marx's dialectical method, and therefore should be accepted or rejected by the same token. The difference lies only in the method of presentation.

Nothing could more clearly reveal the damaging consequences of Rosdolsky's methods than this series of judgements. For while it is quite true from a biographical point of view that Marx's progress towards 'a solution' proceeded via his writing of these sections of the *Grundrisse*, in fact from the point of view of the theoretical content of the texts this development occurred via a complete change of problematic. In the course of the *Grundrisse* itself one can see the birth of one problematic and the elimination of another. The so-called intermediate stages are not just 'left out' of *Capital* as a result of a choice of a method of presentation, but are eliminated as a result of their complete lack of pertinence to the theoretical work of the text. Let us examine this more closely.

In *Capital* the section dealing with the transformation of money into capital is one of the most lucid and theoretically rigorous of the whole book. In this section Marx develops the concept of capital as self-expanding value (by introducing the concepts surplus-value and valorization). Money becomes capital when it becomes self-expanding value in a process represented by the circuit M–C–M'. To use Aristotelian categories, the *potentiality* of the self-expansion of value is given in the concept of money as general equivalent functioning in the circuit of buying and selling. The problem, however, is the conditions for the *actualization* of this potentiality as a real social process. The law of accumulation of capital cannot be derived from the *form* of money alone, but only from an examination of the functioning of monetary transactions within a specific mode of production. Once again here is the difference between 'formal' demonstration and materialist argument based on a realist epistemology.

It is then demonstrated that in this process or circuit the source of the surplus-value cannot be simple commodity exchange. However, the circuit is one which consists of two transactions of buying and selling, that is of two commodity exchanges. So the surplus-value both must be, and yet cannot be, derived from commodity exchange. How can what appears to be a mere trans-forming of value (that is value changing its form, first money, then commodities, then money) result in its expansion? *Formally* the circuit is M–C–M' and there is no general possibility of expansion of value. In the context of certain real social relations, however, the circuit can become M–C–M'. Valorization can occur. How is this possible? 'These are the conditions of the problem. *Hic Rhodus, hic salta!*' (*Capital*, p. 269).

The problem is solved when we recognize within the

sphere of circulation a special commodity 'whose use-value possesses the peculiar property of being a source of value'; this commodity is labour-power. If it were not for the real historical existence of labour-power and of the general framework of capitalist social relations which make this possible, then there would be no self-expansion of value. (In the peculiar ideological situation in which Marxist philosophy finds itself at the present time it is perhaps worth pointing out what ought to be obvious, that the existence of the *concepts* of labour-power and of the capitalist social relations of production would not be sufficient.) Philosophical, speculative considerations cannot give us this solution: both the problem and the solution are based on a realist, materialist epistemology.[10]

Let us compare this with the problem as it is stated in the *Grundrisse*; here, in fact, it is stated in philosophical terms and it receives, before being abandoned unsolved, speculative abstract treatment. The problem with which Marx starts here (*Grundrisse*, pp. 254–5) is that of the *definition* of capital. He produces purely philosophical considerations to show that capital cannot be reduced to exchange or circulation. The concepts of money and the commodity do not *posit* self-renewal: there is nothing inherent in money or commodities in themselves which necessitates a perpetuation of the circuit of exchange. Whereas production 'presupposes circulation as a developed moment' and 'constantly returns from it into itself in order to posit it anew', circulation 'returns back into [production]. It returns into it as into its ground'. The Hegelian origin of this form of demonstration is pointed out in a footnote. Marx continues for many pages to struggle with this problem, that of philosophically specifying the differences between exchange-value and capital, and he eventually arrives back at the point from which he had set out, with the statement that whereas simple exchange-value occurs as both money and as commodities, this dual character is not posited in it: capital, on the other hand, is 'exchange-value posited as the unity of commodity and money, and this positing itself appears as the circulation of capital' (p. 266).

Nothing could be further from the demonstration in

Capital, in which circulation and the valorization of capital are shown to be distinct processes not by reference to what is conceptually posited by what but on the basis of a quantitative consideration of value, and of the different social processes whereby it is either redistributed (circulation) or produced.

In the *Grundrisse* Marx next turns to the consideration of capital as money, and arrives at a definition and proof of capital as self-multiplying value. But this definition and proof are, once again, thoroughly metaphysical in character and, incidentally, utterly unconvincing. He argues (p. 270) that money always exists as both a particular sum and also as the general form of wealth. This alleged formal contradiction (that is it is claimed that there is here a contradiction which derives from *the very form of money*, and not from any considerations of the social processes into which it enters) is the reason why money must 'constantly drive beyond its own barrier', since 'its quantitative limit is in contradiction with its quality', with 'its general concept'. Again (p. 271), 'money as a sum of money is measured by its quantity. This measured-ness contradicts its character, which must be oriented towards the measureless'. A similar argument could be used to show that, since length always exists as both some particular distance between two points on an object and also as the general measure of two-dimensional distances, therefore all material objects must be constantly striving to get longer and to expand to infinity. Speculative demonstration is a truly marvellous form of argument.

This analogy between Marx's speculative demonstration of the self-expansion of money and a formally similar argu-ment for a self-expansion of material objects (which is a *reductio ad absurdum* proof of the invalidity of the former) has been objected to[11] on the grounds that not *all* commodity forms of value self-multiply, but only the general form, money. In fact, however, any material object with the appropriate physical stability and determinateness could function as the general form of length (that is could function as a ruler, or even as the standard unit of measurement) just as any commodity with the appropriate physical properties could function as money. Secondly, it is objected that whereas one cannot, through a process of commensurating lengths, transform a ruler into a length of any other kind of stuff, one can exchange money for any commodity: thus money is not only the standard whereby intercommensurability is made possible but an actual participant in the social process of exchange: it is immediately exchangeable. In fact, however, as the demonstration in *Capital* makes perfectly clear, the immediate and general exchangeability of money for other commodities does *not* in itself prove the concrete possibility of its self-expansion (for how can buying and selling, in which only the form of value is changed, result in a change in its quantity?) but only to its formal potentiality, a potentiality which cannot be actualized except in conditions which are not contained in the money-form itself. This form itself gives rise to a seeming contradiction (precisely that contradiction which the argument in the *Grundrisse* trades upon). This appearance of contradiction is produced precisely because it is *assumed* that both the potentiality and the actualization of self-expansion of money-value are contained in the money-form itself, can be philosophically derived from the money-form itself. The paradox arises from the fact that the social processes which make the self-expansion of value possible, the social relations which are the conditions for valorization, are *hidden* by the money-form. This is another case (formally similar to that discussed in relation to alienation above) where the effective conditions of possibility are displaced, in speculative argument, away from the social relations of production and onto their effects – alienation produces private property in the first case, the money-form produces expansion of value in the second. But unfortunately for philosophy, no examination of the money-form in itself can tell us *where the extra value comes from*. This is the point that is made quite clear in *Capital* but which, in these passages from the *Grundrisse*, has not yet been grasped.

Marx's speculative argument in the *Grundrisse* assigns to particular sums of money some mysterious inner 'drive beyond its own barrier': his argument in *Capital* assigns this drive for self-expansion not to the money-form as such but to the capitalist relations of production, to the existence of the commodity labour-power and to the competition between individual capitals which necessitates accumulation. To repeat, formally one could assert, by analogy, that there is a mysterious inner drive in measuring instruments that makes them expand. In fact, however, in physics, chemistry and biology one studies not the inner drive of rulers to self-expansion but the natural processes whereby things come to be altered in their physical dimensions. On this point the *Grundrisse* is methodologically as far from *Capital* as is mediaeval *impetus* theory from classical physics. The transition to scientific discourse has not yet been accomplished.

If capital is money which constantly strives to go beyond its quantitative limit, how can it achieve this by merely changing *form*, from money to commodities, and back to money? It must, the argument runs, not only change form, it must also negate itself, it must turn into its opposite. But commodities are objectified labour; therefore their opposite is non-objectified labour, labour as subjectivity (p. 272). This is the proof that the self-multiplication of value must pass through the exchange of capital with labour! Again, nothing could be further from the demonstration in *Capital*, in which it is shown that the self-expansion of value requires the purchase of a specific kind of commodity, that is labour-power, the only commodity which has the capacity to create value. At this point in the *Grundrisse* Marx is clearly occupied purely with the formal determination of concepts, and not at all with the social processes of production and distribution of value. His methods of proof and the theorems at which he arrives amply demonstrate the profound difference between this problematic and that of *Capital*. Yet it is precisely at this point in his commentary on the *Grundrisse* that Rosdolsky makes the astonishing remark that here is '*the same solution to the same problem*'. In fact, however, it is neither. It is clear from the subsequent pages of the *Grundrisse* that Marx *could not* at this point in the text have given 'the same solution' to the problem of the transition from money to capital as he was to give in *Capital*. The reason for this is that the distinction between labour and labour-power, which is the key to the solution in *Capital*, had not yet been produced!

When Marx does, later in the *Grundrisse*, at last pose the problem in the same terms as those which appear in *Capital* (that is in terms of quantities of value in the circuit of capital, and that of the source of surplus-value, rather than in terms of the qualitative, conceptual relation between capital and labour conceived as a negation) he poses it as a problem to which he does not yet have the answer. At this point in the text two quite different discourses are juxtaposed. This is the point where one of them is about to cede to the other. Marx's argument is as follows. The act of production cannot simply be the mere reproduction of the value of capital, for 'such a simple preservation of its value contradicts its concept' (p. 316). For capital, 'self-realization includes preservation of the prior value, as well as its multiplication', and this, says Marx, is the *'formal specificity'* of capital (p. 310). But how is it possible for the value to be increased? 'It is easy to understand how labour can increase use-value; the difficulty is, how can it create exchange values greater than those with which it began'. The reason why this is such a puzzle is that the process of production is characterized, in Hegelian terms, as one in which there is change of substance but not of value.

> Capital as a form consists not of objects of labour and labour, but rather of *values*, and, still more precisely, of *prices*. The fact that its value-elements have various substances in common during the production process does not affect their character as values; they are not changed thereby. If, out of the form of unrest – of the process – at the end of the process, they again condense themselves into a resting, objective form, in the product, then this, too, is merely a change of the material in relation to value, and does not alter the latter. (p. 312)

Once again, Hegel's *Science of Logic* is the source of the conceptualization of the problem.

It is only when this metaphysical problematic has been discarded that the problem at last receives its theoretically appropriate expression. The creation of surplus-value is only possible 'if the labour objectified in the price of labour is smaller than the living labour time purchased with it' (p. 321). This formulation of the problem, however, still falls short of terminological and conceptual rigour, and it is only some twenty pages later, with the introduction of the idea of the worker's 'labouring capacity' as the commodity bought by capital, that the solution to the problem emerges. The clear distinction between labour and labour-power, which is at the heart of *Capital*, is present in the later sections of the *Grundrisse* in such formulations as 'the work objectified in the worker's labouring capacity' (that is half a day's work will reproduce a worker with the capacity to work for a whole day – see p. 334). But Marx's difficulty in expressing the relation between labour, 'labouring capacity' and surplus value (pp. 333f) testifies to the fact that this crucial distinction does not stabilize conceptually nor receive definitive terminological expression in the *Grundrisse*.

In this, as in so many other instances, the making of Marx's *Capital* is possible only on condition that Hegel's methods are abandoned. This striking example should be sufficient warning against the temptation to search the *Grundrisse* for the key to Marx's mature scientific work.

VIII

It is normal, in the final section of an essay, to summarize and *conclude*. But I think that given the issues under discussion conclusion would be premature. It seems more appropriate to end not with the appearance of a closure, the achievement of a settled and definitive position, but by pointing out some of the places at which the argument remains most drastically *open*, ready, one hopes, for further development.

The main point of openness, or perhaps of evasion, is in the use of the rather shifting and unsettled terminology with which I have tried to gesture towards certain distinctions. I have pointed, in a way that might stimulate the reader either to irritation or to thought, to some contrasting forms of thought. I have called them, on the one hand, speculative, metaphysical, philosophical, formal, and on the other hand scientific, realist, theoretical. Some *examples* of these contrasting forms of thought have been analysed: they have been presented as raw material on which a certain degree of preliminary work has been done, but it is work which has not resulted in the production of a definitive conceptualization of these distinctions. That remains to be done.

This also means, of course, that the more general questions of the relations between the early and the late works of Marx, and between Marx and Hegel, have not been answered except in relation to some specific, though certainly important, considerations. What I have said should, I think, be taken into account in discussing these questions, but clearly will not in itself settle them. In particular it should be obvious that one central problem has been entirely evaded – the problem of dialectical thought: if there is an Hegelian inheritance in Marx then it will be found to reside in his use of dialectical method. All I have done is to point out what this should *not* be taken to mean, but I have not provided any positive indication as to how to think about Marx's method from this point of view. This essay should be read in conjunction with the others in this present volume and the hope is that taken together they will suggest directions for fruitful future research.

Notes

1   An earlier, shorter version of it, 'The *Grundrisse*: method or metaphysics?', is in *Economy and Society* (November 1978), and is a review article on Roman Rosdolsky's *The Making of Marx's 'Capital'* (London 1977), to which page references are given throughout the present essay.

2   More biographical and historical information about Rosdolsky can be found in Perry Anderson, *Considerations on Western Marxism*, pp. 98–9, and in the notice in *Quatrième Internationale*, no. 33 (1968), to which Anderson refers.

3   Books which approach this status more or less usefully and ambitiously include Kozo Uno, *Principles of Political Economy* (published in Japanese in 1964 and hopefully to be published in an English edition in 1979), and the recent *Le concept de loi économique dans 'le Capital'* by Gérard Dumenil (Paris 1978).

4   I. I. Rubin, *Essays on Marx's Theory of Value* (Detroit 1972).

5   All references to *Capital* are to Vol. I, the Penguin edition, 1976.

6   For a useful and detailed analysis of the differences between the figure of alienation in the *1844 MSS* and that of fetishism in *Capital*, see Nikolas Rose, 'Fetishism and ideology: a review of theoretical problems', *Ideology and Consciousness*, no. 2 (1977). But also see my critical remarks about the philosophical standpoint from which this article is written, in note 8 below.

7   I have myself taken this and other concepts in *Capital* to constitute an implicit *general* theory of ideology at work in Marx's text. It has rightly been pointed out that I did not sufficiently subject this theory to criticism. See 'The Theory of Ideology in *Capital*', reprinted in one of these *Issues in Marxist Philosophy* volumes together with critical comments which point out some of its weaknesses.

8   For contrasting analyses of fetishism see I. I. Rubin's book (note 4 above) where it is taken primarily as functioning within the critique of political economy: Derek Sayer's *Marx's Method: Ideology, Science and Critique in 'Capital'* (Hassocks 1979) in which it is discussed in the context of a general exposition of Marx's materialist and realist theory of science: and Nikolas Rose's article (note 6 above). Rose analyzes the coexistence of different discourses and different figures in *Capital*, but in discussing fetishism he unfortunately does so from within an idealist problematic and is thereby led to overhastily dismiss the possibility that the concept might have useful theoretical content. For he is of the school of those who disdainfully dismiss Marx's realist epistemology as 'empiricist'. See p. 46 of his article for some of the most blatantly idealist formulations of the doctrine that science and ideology do not

differ in their cognitive relation to real objects but only as different discourses with different effects.

9 All page references to the *Grundrisse* are to the Penguin edition, 1973.

10 Clearly my rather militant use of this distinction between 'formal' and 'materialist' argument, and the endorsement of a realist theory of science which is implied, are not provided here with any defence. For arguments in support of these positions see the articles by Collier, Sayer and Bhaskar in Volume III of these *Issues in Marxist Philosophy*. The polemic involved here is of course directed against the idealist and philosophically muddled writings of those in the camp of Hindess and Hirst who, trapped within an Althusserian theoreticism, are still bewitched by the problem of the relation between the real object and the object of thought. For daring to assert that social relations are real and that they are designated by the concepts of Marx's scientific discourse I will no doubt be branded, if it seems worth their time, an empiricist. I regard this polemic as a necessary 'bending of the stick' in a direction opposite to that to which it is forced in the influential works of these sociologists. But while it seems to me appropriate to engage in battle in order to get the epistemological stick to bend one way rather than another at this particular time, I do in fact, in a more serious and less polemical mood, regard the issues involved here as very deep ones, and ones which are not seriously engaged at this rather superficial level of combat. A deeper, and necessarily more anxiety ridden, statement of the philosophical doubts and perplexities raised by these issues can be found in the excellent and courageous work of Cornelius Castoriadis, *Les carrefours du labyrinthe* (Paris 1978).

11 By Chris Arthur, who helpfully commented on this essay.

If you would like to receive regular news on Harvester Press publications, please just send your name and address to our Publicity Department, The Harvester Press Ltd., 17 Ship Street, Brighton, Sussex. We will then be pleased to send you our new announcements and catalogues and special notices of publications in your fields of interest.